Index

Important Notice

These tables cover the main rates of tax announced in the Chancellor's Budget speech on 18 March 2015 and included in the Finance Bill 2015. The rates apply for 2015/16 and for the corporation tax financial year 2015.

How to use these tables for pence

These tables can be used for calculation in £, in pence, or in a combination of £ and pence.

Examples:

Page 6   20% of £28 = £5·60
          20% of 28p = 5·6p = 6p to nearest penny.

Page 17   What is the VAT content at 20% of an inclusive price of £50·83p?

£50·00	=		£8·33
0·83	=	13·83p =	0·14
£50·83	=		£8·47

D1744583

General Editor
Mark McLaughlin CTA (Fellow) ATT (Fellow) TEP, Tax Consultant

Original Contributors
Personal tax
Sarah Laing CTA, Technical Author

Pensions
Alec Ure, Alec Ure & Associates
Tim Webb, TW Pensions Consulting Limited

Corporate tax
Pete Miller CTA (Fellow), Partner, The Miller Partnership
Donald Drysdale CA CTA (Fellow) TEP MBCS CITP, Taxing Words Ltd

VAT
Andrew Needham BA CTA, VAT Specialists Ltd

Customs duties
Jerry Wellens, Equipe Ltd

Property taxes, stamp duty and stamp duty reserve tax
Shimon Shaw, Matthew Arnold & Baldwin LLP

Anti-avoidance
Donald Drysdale CA CTA (Fellow) TEP MBCS CITP, Taxing Words Ltd

HMRC administration
Donald Drysdale CA CTA (Fellow) TEP MBCS CITP, Taxing Words Ltd
Andrew Needham BA CTA, VAT Specialists Ltd
Jerry Wellens, Equipe Ltd

068084273

Bloomsbury Professional

Maxwelton House, 41–43 Boltro Road,
Haywards Heath, West Sussex, RH16 1BJ

© Bloomsbury Professional Ltd 2015.
Bloomsbury Professional, an imprint of Bloomsbury Publishing Plc

ISBN 978 1 78043 889 4

Typeset by Phoenix Photosetting, Chatham, Kent
Printed and bound in Great Britain by CPI Colour

Gifts to Charities – net cost for individuals from 6 April 2015

By donations via Gift Aid and by deduction from pay under the Payroll Giving Schemes.

Gross amount received by Charity	Net cost to Donor Top rate of income tax		Gross amount received by Charity	Net cost to Donor Top rate of income tax	
£	20% £	40% £	£	20% £	40% £
1	0·80	0·60	51	40·80	30·60
2	1·60	1·20	52	41·60	31·20
3	2·40	1·80	53	42·40	31·80
4	3·20	2·40	54	43·20	32·40
5	4·00	3·00	55	44·00	33·00
6	4·80	3·60	56	44·80	33·60
7	5·60	4·20	57	45·60	34·20
8	6·40	4·80	58	46·40	34·80
9	7·20	5·40	59	47·20	35·40
10	8·00	6·00	60	48·00	36·00
11	8·80	6·60	61	48·80	36·60
12	9·60	7·20	62	49·60	37·20
13	10·40	7·80	63	50·40	37·80
14	11·20	8·40	64	51·20	38·40
15	12·00	9·00	65	52·00	39·00
16	12·80	9·60	66	52·80	39·60
17	13·60	10·20	67	53·60	40·20
18	14·40	10·80	68	54·40	40·80
19	15·20	11·40	69	55·20	41·40
20	16·00	12·00	70	56·00	42·00
21	16·80	12·60	71	56·80	42·60
22	17·60	13·20	72	57·60	43·20
23	18·40	13·80	73	58·40	43·80
24	19·20	14·40	74	59·20	44·40
25	20·00	15·00	75	60·00	45·00
26	20·80	15·60	76	60·80	45·60
27	21·60	16·20	77	61·60	46·20
28	22·40	16·80	78	62·40	46·80
29	23·20	17·40	79	63·20	47·40
30	24·00	18·00	80	64·00	48·00
31	24·80	18·60	81	64·80	48·60
32	25·60	19·20	82	65·60	49·20
33	26·40	19·80	83	66·40	49·80
34	27·20	20·40	84	67·20	50·40
35	28·00	21·00	85	68·00	51·00
36	28·80	21·60	86	68·80	51·60
37	29·60	22·20	87	69·60	52·20
38	30·40	22·80	88	70·40	52·80
39	31·20	23·40	89	71·20	53·40
40	32·00	24·00	90	72·00	54·00
41	32·80	24·60	91	72·80	54·60
42	33·60	25·20	92	73·60	55·20
43	34·40	25·80	93	74·40	55·80
44	35·20	26·40	94	75·20	56·40
45	36·00	27·00	95	76·00	57·00
46	36·80	27·60	96	76·80	57·60
47	37·60	28·20	97	77·60	58·20
48	38·40	28·80	98	78·40	58·80
49	39·20	29·40	99	79·20	59·40
50	40·00	30·00	100	80·00	60·00

Net cost to Donor	Gross amount received by Charity, if Donor's top rate of income tax		Net cost to Donor	Gross amount received by Charity, if Donor's top rate of income tax	
£	20% £	40% £	£	20% £	40% £
1	1·25	1·67	51	63·75	85·00
2	2·50	3·33	52	65·00	86·67
3	3·75	5·00	53	66·25	88·33
4	5·00	6·67	54	67·50	90·00
5	6·25	8·33	55	68·75	91·67
6	7·50	10·00	56	70·00	93·33
7	8·75	11·67	57	71·25	95·00
8	10·00	13·33	58	72·50	96·67
9	11·25	15·00	59	73·75	98·33
10	12·50	16·67	60	75·00	100·00
11	13·75	18·33	61	76·25	101·67
12	15·00	20·00	62	77·50	103·33
13	16·25	21·67	63	78·75	105·00
14	17·50	23·33	64	80·00	106·67
15	18·75	25·00	65	81·25	108·33
16	20·00	26·67	66	82·50	110·00
17	21·25	28·33	67	83·75	111·67
18	22·50	30·00	68	85·00	113·33
19	23·75	31·67	69	86·25	115·00
20	25·00	33·33	70	87·50	116·67
21	26·25	35·00	71	88·75	118·33
22	27·50	36·67	72	90·00	120·00
23	28·75	38·33	73	91·25	121·67
24	30·00	40·00	74	92·50	123·33
25	31·25	41·67	75	93·75	125·00
26	32·50	43·33	76	95·00	126·67
27	33·75	45·00	77	96·25	128·33
28	35·00	46·67	78	97·50	130·00
29	36·25	48·33	79	98·75	131·67
30	37·50	50·00	80	100·00	133·33
31	38·75	51·67	81	101·25	135·00
32	40·00	53·33	82	102·50	136·67
33	41·25	55·00	83	103·75	138·33
34	42·50	56·67	84	105·00	140·00
35	43·75	58·33	85	106·25	141·67
36	45·00	60·00	86	107·50	143·33
37	46·25	61·67	87	108·75	145·00
38	47·50	63·33	88	110·00	146·67
39	48·75	65·00	89	111·25	148·33
40	50·00	66·67	90	112·50	150·00
41	51·25	68·33	91	113·75	151·67
42	52·50	70·00	92	115·00	153·33
43	53·75	71·67	93	116·25	155·00
44	55·00	73·33	94	117·50	156·67
45	56·25	75·00	95	118·75	158·33
46	57·50	76·67	96	120·00	160·00
47	58·75	78·33	97	121·25	161·67
48	60·00	80·00	98	122·50	163·33
49	61·25	81·67	99	123·75	165·00
50	62·50	83·33	100	125·00	166·67

10% 2015/16: Rate for capital gains qualifying for Entrepreneurs' Relief

£ or p	Tax £ or p	£ or p	Tax £ or p	£	Tax £	£	Tax £	£	Tax £	£	Tax £	£	Tax £	£	Tax £	£	Tax £	£	Tax £
1	0·10	51	5·10	101	10·10	151	15·10	201	20·10	251	25·10	301	30·10	351	35·10	401	40·10	451	45·10
2	0·20	52	5·20	102	10·20	152	15·20	202	20·20	252	25·20	302	30·20	352	35·20	402	40·20	452	45·20
3	0·30	53	5·30	103	10·30	153	15·30	203	20·30	253	25·30	303	30·30	353	35·30	403	40·30	453	45·30
4	0·40	54	5·40	104	10·40	154	15·40	204	20·40	254	25·40	304	30·40	354	35·40	404	40·40	454	45·40
5	0·50	55	5·50	105	10·50	155	15·50	205	20·50	255	25·50	305	30·50	355	35·50	405	40·50	455	45·50
6	0·60	56	5·60	106	10·60	156	15·60	206	20·60	256	25·60	306	30·60	356	35·60	406	40·60	456	45·60
7	0·70	57	5·70	107	10·70	157	15·70	207	20·70	257	25·70	307	30·70	357	35·70	407	40·70	457	45·70
8	0·80	58	5·80	108	10·80	158	15·80	208	20·80	258	25·80	308	30·80	358	35·80	408	40·80	458	45·80
9	0·90	59	5·90	109	10·90	159	15·90	209	20·90	259	25·90	309	30·90	359	35·90	409	40·90	459	45·90
10	1·00	60	6·00	110	11·00	160	16·00	210	21·00	260	26·00	310	31·00	360	36·00	410	41·00	460	46·00
11	1·10	61	6·10	111	11·10	161	16·10	211	21·10	261	26·10	311	31·10	361	36·10	411	41·10	461	46·10
12	1·20	62	6·20	112	11·20	162	16·20	212	21·20	262	26·20	312	31·20	362	36·20	412	41·20	462	46·20
13	1·30	63	6·30	113	11·30	163	16·30	213	21·30	263	26·30	313	31·30	363	36·30	413	41·30	463	46·30
14	1·40	64	6·40	114	11·40	164	16·40	214	21·40	264	26·40	314	31·40	364	36·40	414	41·40	464	46·40
15	1·50	65	6·50	115	11·50	165	16·50	215	21·50	265	26·50	315	31·50	365	36·50	415	41·50	465	46·50
16	1·60	66	6·60	116	11·60	166	16·60	216	21·60	266	26·60	316	31·60	366	36·60	416	41·60	466	46·60
17	1·70	67	6·70	117	11·70	167	16·70	217	21·70	267	26·70	317	31·70	367	36·70	417	41·70	467	46·70
18	1·80	68	6·80	118	11·80	168	16·80	218	21·80	268	26·80	318	31·80	368	36·80	418	41·80	468	46·80
19	1·90	69	6·90	119	11·90	169	16·90	219	21·90	269	26·90	319	31·90	369	36·90	419	41·90	469	46·90
20	2·00	70	7·00	120	12·00	170	17·00	220	22·00	270	27·00	320	32·00	370	37·00	420	42·00	470	47·00
21	2·10	71	7·10	121	12·10	171	17·10	221	22·10	271	27·10	321	32·10	371	37·10	421	42·10	471	47·10
22	2·20	72	7·20	122	12·20	172	17·20	222	22·20	272	27·20	322	32·20	372	37·20	422	42·20	472	47·20
23	2·30	73	7·30	123	12·30	173	17·30	223	22·30	273	27·30	323	32·30	373	37·30	423	42·30	473	47·30
24	2·40	74	7·40	124	12·40	174	17·40	224	22·40	274	27·40	324	32·40	374	37·40	424	42·40	474	47·40
25	2·50	75	7·50	125	12·50	175	17·50	225	22·50	275	27·50	325	32·50	375	37·50	425	42·50	475	47·50
26	2·60	76	7·60	126	12·60	176	17·60	226	22·60	276	27·60	326	32·60	376	37·60	426	42·60	476	47·60
27	2·70	77	7·70	127	12·70	177	17·70	227	22·70	277	27·70	327	32·70	377	37·70	427	42·70	477	47·70
28	2·80	78	7·80	128	12·80	178	17·80	228	22·80	278	27·80	328	32·80	378	37·80	428	42·80	478	47·80
29	2·90	79	7·90	129	12·90	179	17·90	229	22·90	279	27·90	329	32·90	379	37·90	429	42·90	479	47·90
30	3·00	80	8·00	130	13·00	180	18·00	230	23·00	280	28·00	330	33·00	380	38·00	430	43·00	480	48·00
31	3·10	81	8·10	131	13·10	181	18·10	231	23·10	281	28·10	331	33·10	381	38·10	431	43·10	481	48·10
32	3·20	82	8·20	132	13·20	182	18·20	232	23·20	282	28·20	332	33·20	382	38·20	432	43·20	482	48·20
33	3·30	83	8·30	133	13·30	183	18·30	233	23·30	283	28·30	333	33·30	383	38·30	433	43·30	483	48·30
34	3·40	84	8·40	134	13·40	184	18·40	234	23·40	284	28·40	334	33·40	384	38·40	434	43·40	484	48·40
35	3·50	85	8·50	135	13·50	185	18·50	235	23·50	285	28·50	335	33·50	385	38·50	435	43·50	485	48·50
36	3·60	86	8·60	136	13·60	186	18·60	236	23·60	286	28·60	336	33·60	386	38·60	436	43·60	486	48·60
37	3·70	87	8·70	137	13·70	187	18·70	237	23·70	287	28·70	337	33·70	387	38·70	437	43·70	487	48·70
38	3·80	88	8·80	138	13·80	188	18·80	238	23·80	288	28·80	338	33·80	388	38·80	438	43·80	488	48·80
39	3·90	89	8·90	139	13·90	189	18·90	239	23·90	289	28·90	339	33·90	389	38·90	439	43·90	489	48·90
40	4·00	90	9·00	140	14·00	190	19·00	240	24·00	290	29·00	340	34·00	390	39·00	440	44·00	490	49·00
41	4·10	91	9·10	141	14·10	191	19·10	241	24·10	291	29·10	341	34·10	391	39·10	441	44·10	491	49·10
42	4·20	92	9·20	142	14·20	192	19·20	242	24·20	292	29·20	342	34·20	392	39·20	442	44·20	492	49·20
43	4·30	93	9·30	143	14·30	193	19·30	243	24·30	293	29·30	343	34·30	393	39·30	443	44·30	493	49·30
44	4·40	94	9·40	144	14·40	194	19·40	244	24·40	294	29·40	344	34·40	394	39·40	444	44·40	494	49·40
45	4·50	95	9·50	145	14·50	195	19·50	245	24·50	295	29·50	345	34·50	395	39·50	445	44·50	495	49·50
46	4·60	96	9·60	146	14·60	196	19·60	246	24·60	296	29·60	346	34·60	396	39·60	446	44·60	496	49·60
47	4·70	97	9·70	147	14·70	197	19·70	247	24·70	297	29·70	347	34·70	397	39·70	447	44·70	497	49·70
48	4·80	98	9·80	148	14·80	198	19·80	248	24·80	298	29·80	348	34·80	398	39·80	448	44·80	498	49·80
49	4·90	99	9·90	149	14·90	199	19·90	249	24·90	299	29·90	349	34·90	399	39·90	449	44·90	499	49·90
50	5·00	100	10·00	150	15·00	200	20·00	250	25·00	300	30·00	350	35·00	400	40·00	450	45·00	500	50·00

On Tax	£1,000 £100	£1,500 £150	£2,000 £200	£2,500 £250	£3,000 £300	£3,500 £350	£4,000 £400	£4,500 £450	£5,000 £500

Capital Gains Tax Rate 2015/16   18%

£ or p	Tax £ or p	£ or p	Tax £ or p	£	Tax £	£	Tax £	£	Tax £	£	Tax £	£	Tax £	£	Tax £	£	Tax £	£	Tax £
1	0·18	51	9·18	101	18·18	151	27·18	201	36·18	251	45·18	301	54·18	351	63·18	401	72·18	451	81·18
2	0·36	52	9·36	102	18·36	152	27·36	202	36·36	252	45·36	302	54·36	352	63·36	402	72·36	452	81·36
3	0·54	53	9·54	103	18·54	153	27·54	203	36·54	253	45·54	303	54·54	353	63·54	403	72·54	453	81·54
4	0·72	54	9·72	104	18·72	154	27·72	204	36·72	254	45·72	304	54·72	354	63·72	404	72·72	454	81·72
5	0·90	55	9·90	105	18·90	155	27·90	205	36·90	255	45·90	305	54·90	355	63·90	405	72·90	455	81·90
6	1·08	56	10·08	106	19·08	156	28·08	206	37·08	256	46·08	306	55·08	356	64·08	406	73·08	456	82·08
7	1·26	57	10·26	107	19·26	157	28·26	207	37·26	257	46·26	307	55·26	357	64·26	407	73·26	457	82·26
8	1·44	58	10·44	108	19·44	158	28·44	208	37·44	258	46·44	308	55·44	358	64·44	408	73·44	458	82·44
9	1·62	59	10·62	109	19·62	159	28·62	209	37·62	259	46·62	309	55·62	359	64·62	409	73·62	459	82·62
10	1·80	60	10·80	110	19·80	160	28·80	210	37·80	260	46·80	310	55·80	360	64·80	410	73·80	460	82·80
11	1·98	61	10·98	111	19·98	161	28·98	211	37·98	261	46·98	311	55·98	361	64·98	411	73·98	461	82·98
12	2·16	62	11·16	112	20·16	162	29·16	212	38·16	262	47·16	312	56·16	362	65·16	412	74·16	462	83·16
13	2·34	63	11·34	113	20·34	163	29·34	213	38·34	263	47·34	313	56·34	363	65·34	413	74·34	463	83·34
14	2·52	64	11·52	114	20·52	164	29·52	214	38·52	264	47·52	314	56·52	364	65·52	414	74·52	464	83·52
15	2·70	65	11·70	115	20·70	165	29·70	215	38·70	265	47·70	315	56·70	365	65·70	415	74·70	465	83·70
16	2·88	66	11·88	116	20·88	166	29·88	216	38·88	266	47·88	316	56·88	366	65·88	416	74·88	466	83·88
17	3·06	67	12·06	117	21·06	167	30·06	217	39·06	267	48·06	317	57·06	367	66·06	417	75·06	467	84·06
18	3·24	68	12·24	118	21·24	168	30·24	218	39·24	268	48·24	318	57·24	368	66·24	418	75·24	468	84·24
19	3·42	69	12·42	119	21·42	169	30·42	219	39·42	269	48·42	319	57·42	369	66·42	419	75·42	469	84·42
20	3·60	70	12·60	120	21·60	170	30·60	220	39·60	270	48·60	320	57·60	370	66·60	420	75·60	470	84·60
21	3·78	71	12·78	121	21·78	171	30·78	221	39·78	271	48·78	321	57·78	371	66·78	421	75·78	471	84·78
22	3·96	72	12·96	122	21·96	172	30·96	222	39·96	272	48·96	322	57·96	372	66·96	422	75·96	472	84·96
23	4·14	73	13·14	123	22·14	173	31·14	223	40·14	273	49·14	323	58·14	373	67·14	423	76·14	473	85·14
24	4·32	74	13·32	124	22·32	174	31·32	224	40·32	274	49·32	324	58·32	374	67·32	424	76·32	474	85·32
25	4·50	75	13·50	125	22·50	175	31·50	225	40·50	275	49·50	325	58·50	375	67·50	425	76·50	475	85·50
26	4·68	76	13·68	126	22·68	176	31·68	226	40·68	276	49·68	326	58·68	376	67·68	426	76·68	476	85·68
27	4·86	77	13·86	127	22·86	177	31·86	227	40·86	277	49·86	327	58·86	377	67·86	427	76·86	477	85·86
28	5·04	78	14·04	128	23·04	178	32·04	228	41·04	278	50·04	328	59·04	378	68·04	428	77·04	478	86·04
29	5·22	79	14·22	129	23·22	179	32·22	229	41·22	279	50·22	329	59·22	379	68·22	429	77·22	479	86·22
30	5·40	80	14·40	130	23·40	180	32·40	230	41·40	280	50·40	330	59·40	380	68·40	430	77·40	480	86·40
31	5·58	81	14·58	131	23·58	181	32·58	231	41·58	281	50·58	331	59·58	381	68·58	431	77·58	481	86·58
32	5·76	82	14·76	132	23·76	182	32·76	232	41·76	282	50·76	332	59·76	382	68·76	432	77·76	482	86·76
33	5·94	83	14·94	133	23·94	183	32·94	233	41·94	283	50·94	333	59·94	383	68·94	433	77·94	483	86·94
34	6·12	84	15·12	134	24·12	184	33·12	234	42·12	284	51·12	334	60·12	384	69·12	434	78·12	484	87·12
35	6·30	85	15·30	135	24·30	185	33·30	235	42·30	285	51·30	335	60·30	385	69·30	435	78·30	485	87·30
36	6·48	86	15·48	136	24·48	186	33·48	236	42·48	286	51·48	336	60·48	386	69·48	436	78·48	486	87·48
37	6·66	87	15·66	137	24·66	187	33·66	237	42·66	287	51·66	337	60·66	387	69·66	437	78·66	487	87·66
38	6·84	88	15·84	138	24·84	188	33·84	238	42·84	288	51·84	338	60·84	388	69·84	438	78·84	488	87·84
39	7·02	89	16·02	139	25·02	189	34·02	239	43·02	289	52·02	339	61·02	389	70·02	439	79·02	489	88·02
40	7·20	90	16·20	140	25·20	190	34·20	240	43·20	290	52·20	340	61·20	390	70·20	440	79·20	490	88·20
41	7·38	91	16·38	141	25·38	191	34·38	241	43·38	291	52·38	341	61·38	391	70·38	441	79·38	491	88·38
42	7·56	92	16·56	142	25·56	192	34·56	242	43·56	292	52·56	342	61·56	392	70·56	442	79·56	492	88·56
43	7·74	93	16·74	143	25·74	193	34·74	243	43·74	293	52·74	343	61·74	393	70·74	443	79·74	493	88·74
44	7·92	94	16·92	144	25·92	194	34·92	244	43·92	294	52·92	344	61·92	394	70·92	444	79·92	494	88·92
45	8·10	95	17·10	145	26·10	195	35·10	245	44·10	295	53·10	345	62·10	395	71·10	445	80·10	495	89·10
46	8·28	96	17·28	146	26·28	196	35·28	246	44·28	296	53·28	346	62·28	396	71·28	446	80·28	496	89·28
47	8·46	97	17·46	147	26·46	197	35·46	247	44·46	297	53·46	347	62·46	397	71·46	447	80·46	497	89·46
48	8·64	98	17·64	148	26·64	198	35·64	248	44·64	298	53·64	348	62·64	398	71·64	448	80·64	498	89·64
49	8·82	99	17·82	149	26·82	199	35·82	249	44·82	299	53·82	349	62·82	399	71·82	449	80·82	499	89·82
50	9·00	100	18·00	150	27·00	200	36·00	250	45·00	300	54·00	350	63·00	400	72·00	450	81·00	500	90·00

On Tax	£1,000 £180	£1,500 £270	£2,000 £360	£2,500 £450	£3,000 £540	£3,500 £630	£4,000 £720	£4,500 £810	£5,000 £900

20% Basic Rate 2015/16 Income Tax (a) Corporation Tax

(a) Payable on savings and non-savings income (if 0% band exceeded) up to £31,785.

£ or p	Tax £ or p	£ or p	Tax £ or p	£	Tax £	£	Tax £	£	Tax £	£	Tax £	£	Tax £	£	Tax £	£	Tax £	£	Tax £
1	0·20	51	10·20	101	20·20	151	30·20	201	40·20	251	50·20	301	60·20	351	70·20	401	80·20	451	90·20
2	0·40	52	10·40	102	20·40	152	30·40	202	40·40	252	50·40	302	60·40	352	70·40	402	80·40	452	90·40
3	0·60	53	10·60	103	20·60	153	30·60	203	40·60	253	50·60	303	60·60	353	70·60	403	80·60	453	90·60
4	0·80	54	10·80	104	20·80	154	30·80	204	40·80	254	50·80	304	60·80	354	70·80	404	80·80	454	90·80
5	1·00	55	11·00	105	21·00	155	31·00	205	41·00	255	51·00	305	61·00	355	71·00	405	81·00	455	91·00
6	1·20	56	11·20	106	21·20	156	31·20	206	41·20	256	51·20	306	61·20	356	71·20	406	81·20	456	91·20
7	1·40	57	11·40	107	21·40	157	31·40	207	41·40	257	51·40	307	61·40	357	71·40	407	81·40	457	91·40
8	1·60	58	11·60	108	21·60	158	31·60	208	41·60	258	51·60	308	61·60	358	71·60	408	81·60	458	91·60
9	1·80	59	11·80	109	21·80	159	31·80	209	41·80	259	51·80	309	61·80	359	71·80	409	81·80	459	91·80
10	2·00	60	12·00	110	22·00	160	32·00	210	42·00	260	52·00	310	62·00	360	72·00	410	82·00	460	92·00
11	2·20	61	12·20	111	22·20	161	32·20	211	42·20	261	52·20	311	62·20	361	72·20	411	82·20	461	92·20
12	2·40	62	12·40	112	22·40	162	32·40	212	42·40	262	52·40	312	62·40	362	72·40	412	82·40	462	92·40
13	2·60	63	12·60	113	22·60	163	32·60	213	42·60	263	52·60	313	62·60	363	72·60	413	82·60	463	92·60
14	2·80	64	12·80	114	22·80	164	32·80	214	42·80	264	52·80	314	62·80	364	72·80	414	82·80	464	92·80
15	3·00	65	13·00	115	23·00	165	33·00	215	43·00	265	53·00	315	63·00	365	73·00	415	83·00	465	93·00
16	3·20	66	13·20	116	23·20	166	33·20	216	43·20	266	53·20	316	63·20	366	73·20	416	83·20	466	93·20
17	3·40	67	13·40	117	23·40	167	33·40	217	43·40	267	53·40	317	63·40	367	73·40	417	83·40	467	93·40
18	3·60	68	13·60	118	23·60	168	33·60	218	43·60	268	53·60	318	63·60	368	73·60	418	83·60	468	93·60
19	3·80	69	13·80	119	23·80	169	33·80	219	43·80	269	53·80	319	63·80	369	73·80	419	83·80	469	93·80
20	4·00	70	14·00	120	24·00	170	34·00	220	44·00	270	54·00	320	64·00	370	74·00	420	84·00	470	94·00
21	4·20	71	14·20	121	24·20	171	34·20	221	44·20	271	54·20	321	64·20	371	74·20	421	84·20	471	94·20
22	4·40	72	14·40	122	24·40	172	34·40	222	44·40	272	54·40	322	64·40	372	74·40	422	84·40	472	94·40
23	4·60	73	14·60	123	24·60	173	34·60	223	44·60	273	54·60	323	64·60	373	74·60	423	84·60	473	94·60
24	4·80	74	14·80	124	24·80	174	34·80	224	44·80	274	54·80	324	64·80	374	74·80	424	84·80	474	94·80
25	5·00	75	15·00	125	25·00	175	35·00	225	45·00	275	55·00	325	65·00	375	75·00	425	85·00	475	95·00
26	5·20	76	15·20	126	25·20	176	35·20	226	45·20	276	55·20	326	65·20	376	75·20	426	85·20	476	95·20
27	5·40	77	15·40	127	25·40	177	35·40	227	45·40	277	55·40	327	65·40	377	75·40	427	85·40	477	95·40
28	5·60	78	15·60	128	25·60	178	35·60	228	45·60	278	55·60	328	65·60	378	75·60	428	85·60	478	95·60
29	5·80	79	15·80	129	25·80	179	35·80	229	45·80	279	55·80	329	65·80	379	75·80	429	85·80	479	95·80
30	6·00	80	16·00	130	26·00	180	36·00	230	46·00	280	56·00	330	66·00	380	76·00	430	86·00	480	96·00
31	6·20	81	16·20	131	26·20	181	36·20	231	46·20	281	56·20	331	66·20	381	76·20	431	86·20	481	96·20
32	6·40	82	16·40	132	26·40	182	36·40	232	46·40	282	56·40	332	66·40	382	76·40	432	86·40	482	96·40
33	6·60	83	16·60	133	26·60	183	36·60	233	46·60	283	56·60	333	66·60	383	76·60	433	86·60	483	96·60
34	6·80	84	16·80	134	26·80	184	36·80	234	46·80	284	56·80	334	66·80	384	76·80	434	86·80	484	96·80
35	7·00	85	17·00	135	27·00	185	37·00	235	47·00	285	57·00	335	67·00	385	77·00	435	87·00	485	97·00
36	7·20	86	17·20	136	27·20	186	37·20	236	47·20	286	57·20	336	67·20	386	77·20	436	87·20	486	97·20
37	7·40	87	17·40	137	27·40	187	37·40	237	47·40	287	57·40	337	67·40	387	77·40	437	87·40	487	97·40
38	7·60	88	17·60	138	27·60	188	37·60	238	47·60	288	57·60	338	67·60	388	77·60	438	87·60	488	97·60
39	7·80	89	17·80	139	27·80	189	37·80	239	47·80	289	57·80	339	67·80	389	77·80	439	87·80	489	97·80
40	8·00	90	18·00	140	28·00	190	38·00	240	48·00	290	58·00	340	68·00	390	78·00	440	88·00	490	98·00
41	8·20	91	18·20	141	28·20	191	38·20	241	48·20	291	58·20	341	68·20	391	78·20	441	88·20	491	98·20
42	8·40	92	18·40	142	28·40	192	38·40	242	48·40	292	58·40	342	68·40	392	78·40	442	88·40	492	98·40
43	8·60	93	18·60	143	28·60	193	38·60	243	48·60	293	58·60	343	68·60	393	78·60	443	88·60	493	98·60
44	8·80	94	18·80	144	28·80	194	38·80	244	48·80	294	58·80	344	68·80	394	78·80	444	88·80	494	98·80
45	9·00	95	19·00	145	29·00	195	39·00	245	49·00	295	59·00	345	69·00	395	79·00	445	89·00	495	99·00
46	9·20	96	19·20	146	29·20	196	39·20	246	49·20	296	59·20	346	69·20	396	79·20	446	89·20	496	99·20
47	9·40	97	19·40	147	29·40	197	39·40	247	49·40	297	59·40	347	69·40	397	79·40	447	89·40	497	99·40
48	9·60	98	19·60	148	29·60	198	39·60	248	49·60	298	59·60	348	69·60	398	79·60	448	89·60	498	99·60
49	9·80	99	19·80	149	29·80	199	39·80	249	49·80	299	59·80	349	69·80	399	79·80	449	89·80	499	99·80
50	10·00	100	20·00	150	30·00	200	40·00	250	50·00	300	60·00	350	70·00	400	80·00	450	90·00	500	100·00

| On Tax | | £1,000 £200 | | £1,500 £300 | | £2,000 £400 | | £2,500 £500 | | £3,000 £600 | | £3,500 £700 | | £4,000 £800 | | £4,500 £900 | | £5,000 £1,000 | |

Applies to gains (or part of gains) above the upper limit of the income tax basic rate band. Also applies to trustees and personal representatives.

Higher Rate Capital Gains Tax Rate 28%

£ or p	Tax £ or p	£ or p	Tax £ or p	£	Tax £	£	Tax £	£	Tax £	£	Tax £	£	Tax £	£	Tax £	£	Tax £	£	Tax £
1	0·28	51	14·28	101	28·28	151	42·28	201	56·28	251	70·28	301	84·28	351	8·28	401	112·28	451	126·28
2	0·56	52	14·56	102	28·56	152	42·56	202	56·56	252	70·56	302	84·56	352	8·56	402	112·56	452	126·56
3	0·84	53	14·84	103	28·84	153	42·84	203	56·84	253	70·84	303	84·84	353	8·84	403	112·84	453	126·84
4	1·12	54	15·12	104	29·12	154	43·12	204	57·12	254	71·12	304	85·12	354	9·12	404	113·12	454	127·12
5	1·40	55	15·40	105	29·40	155	43·40	205	57·40	255	71·40	305	85·40	355	9·40	405	113·40	455	127·40
6	1·68	56	15·68	106	29·68	156	43·68	206	57·68	256	71·68	306	85·68	356	9·68	406	113·68	456	127·68
7	1·96	57	15·96	107	29·96	157	43·96	207	57·96	257	71·96	307	85·96	357	9·96	407	113·96	457	127·96
8	2·24	58	16·24	108	30·24	158	44·24	208	58·24	258	72·24	308	86·24	358	100·24	408	114·24	458	128·24
9	2·52	59	16·52	109	30·52	159	44·52	209	58·52	259	72·52	309	86·52	359	100·52	409	114·52	459	128·52
10	2·80	60	16·80	110	30·80	160	44·80	210	58·80	260	72·80	310	86·80	360	100·80	410	114·80	460	128·80
11	3·08	61	17·08	111	31·08	161	45·08	211	59·08	261	73·08	311	87·08	361	101·08	411	115·08	461	129·08
12	3·36	62	17·36	112	31·36	162	45·36	212	59·36	262	73·36	312	87·36	362	101·36	412	115·36	462	129·36
13	3·64	63	17·64	113	31·64	163	45·64	213	59·64	263	73·64	313	87·64	363	101·64	413	115·64	463	129·64
14	3·92	64	17·92	114	31·92	164	45·92	214	59·92	264	73·92	314	87·92	364	101·92	414	115·92	464	129·92
15	4·20	65	18·20	115	32·20	165	46·20	215	60·20	265	74·20	315	88·20	365	102·20	415	116·20	465	130·20
16	4·48	66	18·48	116	32·48	166	46·48	216	60·48	266	74·48	316	88·48	366	102·48	416	116·48	466	130·48
17	4·76	67	18·76	117	32·76	167	46·76	217	60·76	267	74·76	317	88·76	367	102·76	417	116·76	467	130·76
18	5·04	68	19·04	118	33·04	168	47·04	218	61·04	268	75·04	318	89·04	368	103·04	418	117·04	468	131·04
19	5·32	69	19·32	119	33·32	169	47·32	219	61·32	269	75·32	319	89·32	369	103·32	419	117·32	469	131·32
20	5·60	70	19·60	120	33·60	170	47·60	220	61·60	270	75·60	320	89·60	370	103·60	420	117·60	470	131·60
21	5·88	71	19·88	121	33·88	171	47·88	221	61·88	271	75·88	321	89·88	371	103·88	421	117·88	471	131·88
22	6·16	72	20·16	122	34·16	172	48·16	222	62·16	272	76·16	322	90·16	372	104·16	422	118·16	472	132·16
23	6·44	73	20·44	123	34·44	173	48·44	223	62·44	273	76·44	323	90·44	373	104·44	423	118·44	473	132·44
24	6·72	74	20·72	124	34·72	174	48·72	224	62·72	274	76·72	324	90·72	374	104·72	424	118·72	474	132·72
25	7·00	75	21·00	125	35·00	175	49·00	225	63·00	275	77·00	325	91·00	375	105·00	425	119·00	475	133·00
26	7·28	76	21·28	126	35·28	176	49·28	226	63·28	276	77·28	326	91·28	376	105·28	426	119·28	476	133·28
27	7·56	77	21·56	127	35·56	177	49·56	227	63·56	277	77·56	327	91·56	377	105·56	427	119·56	477	133·56
28	7·84	78	21·84	128	35·84	178	49·84	228	63·84	278	77·84	328	91·84	378	105·84	428	119·84	478	133·84
29	8·12	79	22·12	129	36·12	179	50·12	229	64·12	279	78·12	329	92·12	379	106·12	429	120·12	479	134·12
30	8·40	80	22·40	130	36·40	180	50·40	230	64·40	280	78·40	330	92·40	380	106·40	430	120·40	480	134·40
31	8·68	81	22·68	131	36·68	181	50·68	231	64·68	281	78·68	331	92·68	381	106·68	431	120·68	481	134·68
32	8·96	82	22·96	132	36·96	182	50·96	232	64·96	282	78·96	332	92·96	382	106·96	432	120·96	482	134·96
33	9·24	83	23·24	133	37·24	183	51·24	233	65·24	283	79·24	333	93·24	383	107·24	433	121·24	483	135·24
34	9·52	84	23·52	134	37·52	184	51·52	234	65·52	284	79·52	334	93·52	384	107·52	434	121·52	484	135·52
35	9·80	85	23·80	135	37·80	185	51·80	235	65·80	285	79·80	335	93·80	385	107·80	435	121·80	485	135·80
36	10·08	86	24·08	136	38·08	186	52·08	236	66·08	286	80·08	336	94·08	386	108·08	436	122·08	486	136·08
37	10·36	87	24·36	137	38·36	187	52·36	237	66·36	287	80·36	337	94·36	387	108·36	437	122·36	487	136·36
38	10·64	88	24·64	138	38·64	188	52·64	238	66·64	288	80·64	338	94·64	388	108·64	438	122·64	488	136·64
39	10·92	89	24·92	139	38·92	189	52·92	239	66·92	289	80·92	339	94·92	389	108·92	439	122·92	489	136·92
40	11·20	90	25·20	140	39·20	190	53·20	240	67·20	290	81·20	340	95·20	390	109·20	440	123·20	490	137·20
41	11·48	91	25·48	141	39·48	191	53·48	241	67·48	291	81·48	341	95·48	391	109·48	441	123·48	491	137·48
42	11·76	92	25·76	142	39·76	192	53·76	242	67·76	292	81·76	342	95·76	392	109·76	442	123·76	492	137·76
43	12·04	93	26·04	143	40·04	193	54·04	243	68·04	293	82·04	343	96·04	393	110·04	443	124·04	493	138·04
44	12·32	94	26·32	144	40·32	194	54·32	244	68·32	294	82·32	344	96·32	394	110·32	444	124·32	494	138·32
45	12·60	95	26·60	145	40·60	195	54·60	245	68·60	295	82·60	345	96·60	395	110·60	445	124·60	495	138·60
46	12·88	96	26·88	146	40·88	196	54·88	246	68·88	296	82·88	346	96·88	396	110·88	446	124·88	496	138·88
47	13·16	97	27·16	147	41·16	197	55·16	247	69·16	297	83·16	347	97·16	397	111·16	447	125·16	497	139·16
48	13·44	98	27·44	148	41·44	198	55·44	248	69·44	298	83·44	348	97·44	398	111·44	448	125·44	498	139·44
49	13·72	99	27·72	149	41·72	199	55·72	249	69·72	299	83·72	349	97·72	399	111·72	449	125·72	499	139·72
50	14·00	100	28·00	150	42·00	200	56·00	250	70·00	300	84·00	350	98·00	400	112·00	450	126·00	500	140·00

On Tax	£1,000 £280	£1,500 £420	£2,000 £560	£2,500 £700	£3,000 £840	£3,500 £980	£4,000 £1,120	£4,500 £1,260	£5,000 £1,400

32·5%   2015/16: Income Tax on Dividend Income

Payable by higher rate taxpayers on taxable income between £31,786 and £150,000.

£ or p	Tax £ or p	£ or p	Tax £ or p	£	Tax £	£	Tax £	£	Tax £	£	Tax £	£	Tax £	£	Tax £	£	Tax £	£	Tax £
1	0·33	51	16·58	101	32·83	151	49·08	201	65·33	251	81·58	301	97·83	351	114·08	401	130·33	451	146·58
2	0·65	52	16·90	102	33·15	152	49·40	202	65·65	252	81·90	302	98·15	352	114·40	402	130·65	452	146·90
3	0·98	53	17·23	103	33·48	153	49·73	203	65·98	253	82·23	303	98·48	353	114·73	403	130·98	453	147·23
4	1·30	54	17·55	104	33·80	154	50·05	204	66·30	254	82·55	304	98·80	354	115·05	404	131·30	454	147·55
5	1·63	55	17·88	105	34·13	155	50·38	205	66·63	255	82·88	305	99·13	355	115·38	405	131·63	455	147·88
6	1·95	56	18·20	106	34·45	156	50·70	206	66·95	256	83·20	306	99·45	356	115·70	406	131·95	456	148·20
7	2·28	57	18·53	107	34·78	157	51·03	207	67·28	257	83·53	307	99·78	357	116·03	407	132·28	457	148·53
8	2·60	58	18·85	108	35·10	158	51·35	208	67·60	258	83·85	308	100·10	358	116·35	408	132·60	458	148·85
9	2·93	59	19·18	109	35·43	159	51·68	209	67·93	259	84·18	309	100·43	359	116·68	409	132·93	459	149·18
10	3·25	60	19·50	110	35·75	160	52·00	210	68·25	260	84·50	310	100·75	360	117·00	410	133·25	460	149·50
11	3·58	61	19·83	111	36·08	161	52·33	211	68·58	261	84·83	311	101·08	361	117·33	411	133·58	461	149·83
12	3·90	62	20·15	112	36·40	162	52·65	212	68·90	262	85·15	312	101·40	362	117·65	412	133·90	462	150·15
13	4·23	63	20·48	113	36·73	163	52·98	213	69·23	263	85·48	313	101·73	363	117·98	413	134·23	463	150·48
14	4·55	64	20·80	114	37·05	164	53·30	214	69·55	264	85·80	314	102·05	364	118·30	414	134·55	464	150·80
15	4·88	65	21·13	115	37·38	165	53·63	215	69·88	265	86·13	315	102·38	365	118·63	415	134·88	465	151·13
16	5·20	66	21·45	116	37·70	166	53·95	216	70·20	266	86·45	316	102·70	366	118·95	416	135·20	466	151·45
17	5·53	67	21·78	117	38·03	167	54·28	217	70·53	267	86·78	317	103·03	367	119·28	417	135·53	467	151·78
18	5·85	68	22·10	118	38·35	168	54·60	218	70·85	268	87·10	318	103·35	368	119·60	418	135·85	468	152·10
19	6·18	69	22·43	119	38·68	169	54·93	219	71·18	269	87·43	319	103·68	369	119·93	419	136·18	469	152·43
20	6·50	70	22·75	120	39·00	170	55·25	220	71·50	270	87·75	320	104·00	370	120·25	420	136·50	470	152·75
21	6·83	71	23·08	121	39·33	171	55·58	221	71·83	271	88·08	321	104·33	371	120·58	421	136·83	471	153·08
22	7·15	72	23·40	122	39·65	172	55·90	222	72·15	272	88·40	322	104·65	372	120·90	422	137·15	472	153·40
23	7·48	73	23·73	123	39·98	173	56·23	223	72·48	273	88·73	323	104·98	373	121·23	423	137·48	473	153·73
24	7·80	74	24·05	124	40·30	174	56·55	224	72·80	274	89·05	324	105·30	374	121·55	424	137·80	474	154·05
25	8·13	75	24·38	125	40·63	175	56·88	225	73·13	275	89·38	325	105·63	375	121·88	425	138·13	475	154·38
26	8·45	76	24·70	126	40·95	176	57·20	226	73·45	276	89·70	326	105·95	376	122·20	426	138·45	476	154·70
27	8·78	77	25·03	127	41·28	177	57·53	227	73·78	277	90·03	327	106·28	377	122·53	427	138·78	477	155·03
28	9·10	78	25·35	128	41·60	178	57·85	228	74·10	278	90·35	328	106·60	378	122·85	428	139·10	478	155·35
29	9·43	79	25·68	129	41·93	179	58·18	229	74·43	279	90·68	329	106·93	379	123·18	429	139·43	479	155·68
30	9·75	80	26·00	130	42·25	180	58·50	230	74·75	280	91·00	330	107·25	380	123·50	430	139·75	480	156·00
31	10·08	81	26·33	131	42·58	181	58·83	231	75·08	281	91·33	331	107·58	381	123·83	431	140·08	481	156·33
32	10·40	82	26·65	132	42·90	182	59·15	232	75·40	282	91·65	332	107·90	382	124·15	432	140·40	482	156·65
33	10·73	83	26·98	133	43·23	183	59·48	233	75·73	283	91·98	333	108·23	383	124·48	433	140·73	483	156·98
34	11·05	84	27·30	134	43·55	184	59·80	234	76·05	284	92·30	334	108·55	384	124·80	434	141·05	484	157·30
35	11·38	85	27·63	135	43·88	185	60·13	235	76·38	285	92·63	335	108·88	385	125·13	435	141·38	485	157·63
36	11·70	86	27·95	136	44·20	186	60·45	236	76·70	286	92·95	336	109·20	386	125·45	436	141·70	486	157·95
37	12·03	87	28·28	137	44·53	187	60·78	237	77·03	287	93·28	337	109·53	387	125·78	437	142·03	487	158·28
38	12·35	88	28·60	138	44·85	188	61·10	238	77·35	288	93·60	338	109·85	388	126·10	438	142·35	488	158·60
39	12·68	89	28·93	139	45·18	189	61·43	239	77·68	289	93·93	339	110·18	389	126·43	439	142·68	489	158·93
40	13·00	90	29·25	140	45·50	190	61·75	240	78·00	290	94·25	340	110·50	390	126·75	440	143·00	490	159·25
41	13·33	91	29·58	141	45·83	191	62·08	241	78·33	291	94·58	341	110·83	391	127·08	441	143·33	491	159·58
42	13·65	92	29·90	142	46·15	192	62·40	242	78·65	292	94·90	342	111·15	392	127·40	442	143·65	492	159·90
43	13·98	93	30·23	143	46·48	193	62·73	243	78·98	293	95·23	343	111·48	393	127·73	443	143·98	493	160·23
44	14·30	94	30·55	144	46·80	194	63·05	244	79·30	294	95·55	344	111·80	394	128·05	444	144·30	494	160·55
45	14·63	95	30·88	145	47·13	195	63·38	245	79·63	295	95·88	345	112·13	395	128·38	445	144·63	495	160·88
46	14·95	96	31·20	146	47·45	196	63·70	246	79·95	296	96·20	346	112·45	396	128·70	446	144·95	496	161·20
47	15·28	97	31·53	147	47·78	197	64·03	247	80·28	297	96·53	347	112·78	397	129·03	447	145·28	497	161·53
48	15·60	98	31·85	148	48·10	198	64·35	248	80·60	298	96·85	348	113·10	398	129·35	448	145·60	498	161·85
49	15·93	99	32·18	149	48·43	199	64·68	249	80·93	299	97·18	349	113·43	399	129·68	449	145·93	499	162·18
50	16·25	100	32·50	150	48·75	200	65·00	250	81·25	300	97·50	350	113·75	400	130·00	450	146·25	500	162·50

On Tax	£1,000 £325	£1,500 £488	£2,000 £650	£2,500 £813	£3,000 £975	£3,500 £1,138	£4,000 £1,300	£4,500 £1,463	£5,000 £1,625

Payable by higher rate taxpayers on taxable income between £31,786 and £150,000.

2015/16: Income Tax on Dividend Income   32·5%

£ or p	Tax £ or p	£ or p	Tax £ or p	£	Tax £	£	Tax £	£	Tax £	£	Tax £	£	Tax £	£	Tax £	£	Tax £	£	Tax £
501	162·83	551	179·08	601	195·33	651	211·58	701	227·83	751	244·08	801	260·33	851	276·58	901	292·83	951	309·08
502	163·15	552	179·40	602	195·65	652	211·90	702	228·15	752	244·40	802	260·65	852	276·90	902	293·15	952	309·40
503	163·48	553	179·73	603	195·98	653	212·23	703	228·48	753	244·73	803	260·98	853	277·23	903	293·48	953	309·73
504	163·80	554	180·05	604	196·30	654	212·55	704	228·80	754	245·05	804	261·30	854	277·55	904	293·80	954	310·05
505	164·13	555	180·38	605	196·63	655	212·88	705	229·13	755	245·38	805	261·63	855	277·88	905	294·13	955	310·38
506	164·45	556	180·70	606	196·95	656	213·20	706	229·45	756	245·70	806	261·95	856	278·20	906	294·45	956	310·70
507	164·78	557	181·03	607	197·28	657	213·53	707	229·78	757	246·03	807	262·28	857	278·53	907	294·78	957	311·03
508	165·10	558	181·35	608	197·60	658	213·85	708	230·10	758	246·35	808	262·60	858	278·85	908	295·10	958	311·35
509	165·43	559	181·68	609	197·93	659	214·18	709	230·43	759	246·68	809	262·93	859	279·18	909	295·43	959	311·68
510	165·75	560	182·00	610	198·25	660	214·50	710	230·75	760	247·00	810	263·25	860	279·50	910	295·75	960	312·00
511	166·08	561	182·33	611	198·58	661	214·83	711	231·08	761	247·33	811	263·58	861	279·83	911	296·08	961	312·33
512	166·40	562	182·65	612	198·90	662	215·15	712	231·40	762	247·65	812	263·90	862	280·15	912	296·40	962	312·65
513	166·73	563	182·98	613	199·23	663	215·48	713	231·73	763	247·98	813	264·23	863	280·48	913	296·73	963	312·98
514	167·05	564	183·30	614	199·55	664	215·80	714	232·05	764	248·30	814	264·55	864	280·80	914	297·05	964	313·30
515	167·38	565	183·63	615	199·88	665	216·13	715	232·38	765	248·63	815	264·88	865	281·13	915	297·38	965	313·63
516	167·70	566	183·95	616	200·20	666	216·45	716	232·70	766	248·95	816	265·20	866	281·45	916	297·70	966	313·95
517	168·03	567	184·28	617	200·53	667	216·78	717	233·03	767	249·28	817	265·53	867	281·78	917	298·03	967	314·28
518	168·35	568	184·60	618	200·85	668	217·10	718	233·35	768	249·60	818	265·85	868	282·10	918	298·35	968	314·60
519	168·68	569	184·93	619	201·18	669	217·43	719	233·68	769	249·93	819	266·18	869	282·43	919	298·68	969	314·93
520	169·00	570	185·25	620	201·50	670	217·75	720	234·00	770	250·25	820	266·50	870	282·75	920	299·00	970	315·25
521	169·33	571	185·58	621	201·83	671	218·08	721	234·33	771	250·58	821	266·83	871	283·08	921	299·33	971	315·58
522	169·65	572	185·90	622	202·15	672	218·40	722	234·65	772	250·90	822	267·15	872	283·40	922	299·65	972	315·90
523	169·98	573	186·23	623	202·48	673	218·73	723	234·98	773	251·23	823	267·48	873	283·73	923	299·98	973	316·23
524	170·30	574	186·55	624	202·80	674	219·05	724	235·30	774	251·55	824	267·80	874	284·05	924	300·30	974	316·55
525	170·63	575	186·88	625	203·13	675	219·38	725	235·63	775	251·88	825	268·13	875	284·38	925	300·63	975	316·88
526	170·95	576	187·20	626	203·45	676	219·70	726	235·95	776	252·20	826	268·45	876	284·70	926	300·95	976	317·20
527	171·28	577	187·53	627	203·78	677	220·03	727	236·28	777	252·53	827	268·78	877	285·03	927	301·28	977	317·53
528	171·60	578	187·85	628	204·10	678	220·35	728	236·60	778	252·85	828	269·10	878	285·35	928	301·60	978	317·85
529	171·93	579	188·18	629	204·43	679	220·68	729	236·93	779	253·18	829	269·43	879	285·68	929	301·93	979	318·18
530	172·25	580	188·50	630	204·75	680	221·00	730	237·25	780	253·50	830	269·75	880	286·00	930	302·25	980	318·50
531	172·58	581	188·83	631	205·08	681	221·33	731	237·58	781	253·83	831	270·08	881	286·33	931	302·58	981	318·83
532	172·90	582	189·15	632	205·40	682	221·65	732	237·90	782	254·15	832	270·40	882	286·65	932	302·90	982	319·15
533	173·23	583	189·48	633	205·73	683	221·98	733	238·23	783	254·48	833	270·73	883	286·98	933	303·23	983	319·48
534	173·55	584	189·80	634	206·05	684	222·30	734	238·55	784	254·80	834	271·05	884	287·30	934	303·55	984	319·80
535	173·88	585	190·13	635	206·38	685	222·63	735	238·88	785	255·13	835	271·38	885	287·63	935	303·88	985	320·13
536	174·20	586	190·45	636	206·70	686	222·95	736	239·20	786	255·45	836	271·70	886	287·95	936	304·20	986	320·45
537	174·53	587	190·78	637	207·03	687	223·28	737	239·53	787	255·78	837	272·03	887	288·28	937	304·53	987	320·78
538	174·85	588	191·10	638	207·35	688	223·60	738	239·85	788	256·10	838	272·35	888	288·60	938	304·85	988	321·10
539	175·18	589	191·43	639	207·68	689	223·93	739	240·18	789	256·43	839	272·68	889	288·93	939	305·18	989	321·43
540	175·50	590	191·75	640	208·00	690	224·25	740	240·50	790	256·75	840	273·00	890	289·25	940	305·50	990	321·75
541	175·83	591	192·08	641	208·33	691	224·58	741	240·83	791	257·08	841	273·33	891	289·58	941	305·83	991	322·08
542	176·15	592	192·40	642	208·65	692	224·90	742	241·15	792	257·40	842	273·65	892	289·90	942	306·15	992	322·40
543	176·48	593	192·73	643	208·98	693	225·23	743	241·48	793	257·73	843	273·98	893	290·23	943	306·48	993	322·73
544	176·80	594	193·05	644	209·30	694	225·55	744	241·80	794	258·05	844	274·30	894	290·55	944	306·80	994	323·05
545	177·13	595	193·38	645	209·63	695	225·88	745	242·13	795	258·38	845	274·63	895	290·88	945	307·13	995	323·38
546	177·45	596	193·70	646	209·95	696	226·20	746	242·45	796	258·70	846	274·95	896	291·20	946	307·45	996	323·70
547	177·78	597	194·03	647	210·28	697	226·53	747	242·78	797	259·03	847	275·28	897	291·53	947	307·78	997	324·03
548	178·10	598	194·35	648	210·60	698	226·85	748	243·10	798	259·35	848	275·60	898	291·85	948	308·10	998	324·35
549	178·43	599	194·68	649	210·93	699	227·18	749	243·43	799	259·68	849	275·93	899	292·18	949	308·43	999	324·68
550	178·75	600	195·00	650	211·25	700	227·50	750	243·75	800	260·00	850	276·25	900	292·50	950	308·75	1000	325·00

| On Tax | £5,500 £1,788 | £6,000 £1,950 | £6,500 £2,113 | £7,000 £2,275 | £7,500 £2,438 | £8,000 £2,600 | £8,500 £2,763 | £9,000 £2,925 | £9,500 £3,088 |

37·5% 2015/16: Dividend Additional Rate (a)
Dividend Trust Rate (b)

(a) Payable on dividends otherwise taxable at the additional rate
(b) Dividend trust rate

£ or p	Tax £ or p	£ or p	Tax £ or p	£	Tax £	£	Tax £	£	Tax £	£	Tax £	£	Tax £	£	Tax £	£	Tax £	£	Tax £
1	0·38	51	19·13	101	37·88	151	56·63	201	75·38	251	94·13	301	112·88	351	131·63	401	150·38	451	169·13
2	0·75	52	19·50	102	38·25	152	57·00	202	75·75	252	94·50	302	113·25	352	132·00	402	150·75	452	169·50
3	1·13	53	19·88	103	38·63	153	57·38	203	76·13	253	94·88	303	113·63	353	132·38	403	151·13	453	169·88
4	1·50	54	20·25	104	39·00	154	57·75	204	76·50	254	95·25	304	114·00	354	132·75	404	151·50	454	170·25
5	1·88	55	20·63	105	39·38	155	58·13	205	76·88	255	95·63	305	114·38	355	133·13	405	151·88	455	170·63
6	2·25	56	21·00	106	39·75	156	58·50	206	77·25	256	96·00	306	114·75	356	133·50	406	152·25	456	171·00
7	2·63	57	21·38	107	40·13	157	58·88	207	77·63	257	96·38	307	115·13	357	133·88	407	152·63	457	171·38
8	3·00	58	21·75	108	40·50	158	59·25	208	78·00	258	96·75	308	115·50	358	134·25	408	153·00	458	171·75
9	3·38	59	22·13	109	40·88	159	59·63	209	78·38	259	97·13	309	115·88	359	134·63	409	153·38	459	172·13
10	3·75	60	22·50	110	41·25	160	60·00	210	78·75	260	97·50	310	116·25	360	135·00	410	153·75	460	172·50
11	4·13	61	22·88	111	41·63	161	60·38	211	79·13	261	97·88	311	116·63	361	135·38	411	154·13	461	172·88
12	4·50	62	23·25	112	42·00	162	60·75	212	79·50	262	98·25	312	117·00	362	135·75	412	154·50	462	173·25
13	4·88	63	23·63	113	42·38	163	61·13	213	79·88	263	98·63	313	117·38	363	136·13	413	154·88	463	173·63
14	5·25	64	24·00	114	42·75	164	61·50	214	80·25	264	99·00	314	117·75	364	136·50	414	155·25	464	174·00
15	5·63	65	24·38	115	43·13	165	61·88	215	80·63	265	99·38	315	118·13	365	136·88	415	155·63	465	174·38
16	6·00	66	24·75	116	43·50	166	62·25	216	81·00	266	99·75	316	118·50	366	137·25	416	156·00	466	174·75
17	6·38	67	25·13	117	43·88	167	62·63	217	81·38	267	100·13	317	118·88	367	137·63	417	156·38	467	175·13
18	6·75	68	25·50	118	44·25	168	63·00	218	81·75	268	100·50	318	119·25	368	138·00	418	156·75	468	175·50
19	7·13	69	25·88	119	44·63	169	63·38	219	82·13	269	100·88	319	119·63	369	138·38	419	157·13	469	175·88
20	7·50	70	26·25	120	45·00	170	63·75	220	82·50	270	101·25	320	120·00	370	138·75	420	157·50	470	176·25
21	7·88	71	26·63	121	45·38	171	64·13	221	82·88	271	101·63	321	120·38	371	139·13	421	157·88	471	176·63
22	8·25	72	27·00	122	45·75	172	64·50	222	83·25	272	102·00	322	120·75	372	139·50	422	158·25	472	177·00
23	8·63	73	27·38	123	46·13	173	64·88	223	83·63	273	102·38	323	121·13	373	139·88	423	158·63	473	177·38
24	9·00	74	27·75	124	46·50	174	65·25	224	84·00	274	102·75	324	121·50	374	140·25	424	159·00	474	177·75
25	9·38	75	28·13	125	46·88	175	65·63	225	84·38	275	103·13	325	121·88	375	140·63	425	159·38	475	178·13
26	9·75	76	28·50	126	47·25	176	66·00	226	84·75	276	103·50	326	122·25	376	141·00	426	159·75	476	178·50
27	10·13	77	28·88	127	47·63	177	66·38	227	85·13	277	103·88	327	122·63	377	141·38	427	160·13	477	178·88
28	10·50	78	29·25	128	48·00	178	66·75	228	85·50	278	104·25	328	123·00	378	141·75	428	160·50	478	179·25
29	10·88	79	29·63	129	48·38	179	67·13	229	85·88	279	104·63	329	123·38	379	142·13	429	160·88	479	179·63
30	11·25	80	30·00	130	48·75	180	67·50	230	86·25	280	105·00	330	123·75	380	142·50	430	161·25	480	180·00
31	11·63	81	30·38	131	49·13	181	67·88	231	86·63	281	105·38	331	124·13	381	142·88	431	161·63	481	180·38
32	12·00	82	30·75	132	49·50	182	68·25	232	87·00	282	105·75	332	124·50	382	143·25	432	162·00	482	180·75
33	12·38	83	31·13	133	49·88	183	68·63	233	87·38	283	106·13	333	124·88	383	143·63	433	162·38	483	181·13
34	12·75	84	31·50	134	50·25	184	69·00	234	87·75	284	106·50	334	125·25	384	144·00	434	162·75	484	181·50
35	13·13	85	31·88	135	50·63	185	69·38	235	88·13	285	106·88	335	125·63	385	144·38	435	163·13	485	181·88
36	13·50	86	32·25	136	51·00	186	69·75	236	88·50	286	107·25	336	126·00	386	144·75	436	163·50	486	182·25
37	13·88	87	32·63	137	51·38	187	70·13	237	88·88	287	107·63	337	126·38	387	145·13	437	163·88	487	182·63
38	14·25	88	33·00	138	51·75	188	70·50	238	89·25	288	108·00	338	126·75	388	145·50	438	164·25	488	183·00
39	14·63	89	33·38	139	52·13	189	70·88	239	89·63	289	108·38	339	127·13	389	145·88	439	164·63	489	183·38
40	15·00	90	33·75	140	52·50	190	71·25	240	90·00	290	108·75	340	127·50	390	146·25	440	165·00	490	183·75
41	15·38	91	34·13	141	52·88	191	71·63	241	90·38	291	109·13	341	127·88	391	146·63	441	165·38	491	184·13
42	15·75	92	34·50	142	53·25	192	72·00	242	90·75	292	109·50	342	128·25	392	147·00	442	165·75	492	184·50
43	16·13	93	34·88	143	53·63	193	72·38	243	91·13	293	109·88	343	128·63	393	147·38	443	166·13	493	184·88
44	16·50	94	35·25	144	54·00	194	72·75	244	91·50	294	110·25	344	129·00	394	147·75	444	166·50	494	185·25
45	16·88	95	35·63	145	54·38	195	73·13	245	91·88	295	110·63	345	129·38	395	148·13	445	166·88	495	185·63
46	17·25	96	36·00	146	54·75	196	73·50	246	92·25	296	111·00	346	129·75	396	148·50	446	167·25	496	186·00
47	17·63	97	36·38	147	55·13	197	73·88	247	92·63	297	111·38	347	130·13	397	148·88	447	167·63	497	186·38
48	18·00	98	36·75	148	55·50	198	74·25	248	93·00	298	111·75	348	130·50	398	149·25	448	168·00	498	186·75
49	18·38	99	37·13	149	55·88	199	74·63	249	93·38	299	112·13	349	130·88	399	149·63	449	168·38	499	187·13
50	18·75	100	37·50	150	56·25	200	75·00	250	93·75	300	112·50	350	131·25	400	150·00	450	168·75	500	187·50

| On Tax | | £1,000 £375 | | £1,500 £563 | | £2,000 £750 | | £2,500 £938 | | £3,000 £1,125 | | £3,500 £1,313 | | £4,000 £1,500 | | £4,500 £1,688 | | £5,000 £1,875 | |

The Budget proposals are introduced by the Chancellor of the Exchequer in the House of Commons.
Note: Please remember that these proposals are subject to amendment during the passage of the Finance Bill through Parliament.

Allowances

	2014/15 (£)	2015/16 (£)
Personal allowance for people born after 5 April 1948	10,000	10,600
Income limit for personal allowance (reduces by £1 for every £2 where income is over £100,000, irrespective of age)	100,000	100,000
Abatement income ceiling for personal allowances	120,000	121,200
Personal allowance for people born between 6 April 1938 and 5 April 1948	10,500	10,600
Personal allowance for people born before 6 April 1938	10,660	10,660
Married couples allowance – born before 6 April 1935 (10% relief)	8,165	8,355
Income limit for allowances for those born before 6 April 1948	27,000	27,700
Minimum Married couple's allowance	3,140	3,220
Blind person's allowance	2,230	2,290

Income Tax rates

	2014/15	2015/16
Rate on non-dividend savings income	10%	0%
On taxable income up to	2,880*	5,000*

*Starting rate applies to savings income only. If non-savings income is above this limit then the starting rate for savings does not apply.

Basic rate	20%	20%
On taxable income up to	31,865	31,785
Higher rate	40%	40%
On taxable income over	31,865	31,785
Additional rate	45%	45%
On taxable income over	150,000	150,000
Lower rate on dividend income	10%	10%
Higher rate on dividend income	32.50%	32.50%
Additional higher rate	37.50%	37.50%

Company taxation

	FY2014	FY2015
Corporation tax rates		
Main rate	21%	20%
Companies with small profits	20%	N/A
– 20% rate limit	£300,000	N/A
– marginal relief limit	£1,500,000	N/A
– marginal rate	21.25%	N/A
Standard fraction	1/400	N/A

Capital gains

	2014/15	2015/16
Rates		
– Individuals	18%/28%*	18%/28%*
– Trustees and personal representatives	28%	28%
– Entreprenuers' relief flat rate	10%	10%
General exemption limit	11,000	11,100

* Chargeable gains are aggregated with taxable income and to the extent that the aggregate falls above the income tax basic rate threshold, CGT is charged at 28% (taking the chargeable gains as being the highest part of that aggregate). If the aggregate falls below the threshold, the CGT rate will be 18%.

Inheritance tax

Threshold (year from 6/4/2015)	£325,000
Death rate	40%

VAT

Standard rate	20%
Registration threshold from 1 April 2015 (previously £81,000 from 1 April 2014)	82,000

National Insurance

	2014/15	2015/16
	£ per week	£ per week
Class 1		
Lower earnings limit – primary	111	112
Upper earnings limit – primary	805	815
Upper accrual point	770	770
Primary threshold	153	155
Secondary threshold	153	156
Employee contributution rate between primary and upper earnings limit	12%	12%
Employee contributution rate above upper earnings limit	2%	2%
Empoyees' contracted-out rebate (COSRs)	1.40%	1.40%
Employers' secondary rate above secondary threshold	13.80%	13.80%
Employers' contracted-out rebate (salary-related schemes)	3.40%	3.40%
Class 1A and 1B	13.80%	13.80%
Class 2		
Flat weekly rate	£2.75	£2.80
Exemption limit	£5,885	£5,965
Class 3		
Flat weekly rate	£13.90	£14.10
Class 4		
Lower profits limit	£7,956	£8,060
Upper profits limit	£41,865	£42,385
Rate payable between lower and upper profits limits	9%	9%
Rate payable on profits over upper profits limit	2%	2%

Summary of Budget Proposals 18 March 2015

Income tax, etc

Income tax: personal allowance for those born after 5 April 1938 for 2015/16

For 2015/16, the personal allowance for those born after 5 April 1938 will be increased to £10,600, and the basic rate threshold will be reduced to £31,785.

Income tax: personal allowance and basic rate limit for 2016/17 and 2017/18

The personal allowance will be increased to £10,800 for 2016/17, and £11,000 for 2017/18. The basic rate limit will be increased to £31,900 for 2016/17, and £32,300 for 2017/18. The higher rate threshold will be £42,700 in 2016/17, and £43,300 in 2017/18.

From 2016/17, there will be one income tax personal allowance, regardless of an individual's date of birth.

Blind person's allowance, married couple's allowance and income limit for 2015/16

Blind person's allowance is set at £2,290 for 2015/16. For 2015/16, maximum married couple's allowance available will rise from £8,165 to £8,355. Minimum married couple's allowance will also rise from £3,140 to £3,220. The income limit for the abatement of personal allowances will rise from £27,000 in 2014/15 to £27,700 in 2015/16.

Income tax: company car tax rates and bands for cars 2017/18 and 2018/19

In both 2017/18 and 2018/19, the appropriate percentage of the list price of company cars subject to tax will increase by two percentage points for cars emitting more than 75g of carbon dioxide (CO_2) per kilometre (km).

In 2017/18, there will be a four-percentage point differential between the 0–50 and 51–75g CO_2 per km bands, and between the 51–75 and 76–94g CO_2 per km bands. In 2018/19, the differential in each case will reduce to three percentage points.

The differential is set to reduce further to two percentage points in 2019/20, in line with the Budget 2013 announcement.

Legislation will be introduced in Finance Bill 2015 to make the following changes:

- From 6 April 2017, the graduated table of company car tax bands will provide for a 9% band for cars with emissions of 0–50g CO_2 per km; a 13% band for cars with emissions of 51–75g CO_2 per km; a 17% band for other low emission cars (76g–94g CO_2 per km); and a 2% increase for each rise in emissions of 5g CO_2 per kg from 95g CO_2 to the existing maximum of 37%.
- From 6 April 2018, there will be a 13% band for cars with emissions of 0–50g CO_2 per km; a 16% band for cars with emissions of 51–75g CO_2 per km; a 19% band for other low emission cars (76g–94g CO_2 per km); and a 2% increase for each rise in emissions of 5g CO_2 per km from 95g CO_2 to the existing maximum of 37%.
- From 6 April 2017, the appropriate percentage for cars with a cylinder capacity of up 1,400cc will be set at 18% (rising to 20% from 6 April 2018); for cars between 1,401cc and 2,000cc, the appropriate percentage will be 29% (rising to 31% from 6 April 2018); and for those over 2,000cc the percentage will remain at 37%.
- From 6 April 2015, the maximum percentage for diesel cars will be 37%. From 6 April 2017, the appropriate percentage for diesel cars will follow in line with those for petrol cars outlined above.

Income tax: van benefit charge for zero emission vans

From tax year 2015/16, a rate of 20% of the van benefit charge for vans which emit CO_2 will apply to zero-emission vans. This rate will increase each year as follows, until it is equivalent to 100% of the van benefit charge for vans which emit CO_2:

- 40% in 2016/17;
- 60% in 2017/18;
- 80% in 2018/19;
- 90% in 2019/20; and
- 100% in 2020/21.

The changes mean that from 2020/21 onwards, the van benefit charge for zero emission vans will be the same as the van benefit charge for vans which emit CO_2.

For vans which emit CO_2, the existing van benefit charge continues to apply. The cash equivalent of the van benefit charge remains at nil where the restricted private use condition is met.

Income tax: abolition of the £8,500 threshold for benefits-in-kind

The £8,500 threshold that determines whether employees pay income tax on all of their benefits in kind and expenses is to be abolished from 6 April 2016.

From April 2016, employers will have additional National Insurance contributions to pay on the benefits and certain expenses provided to employees earning at a rate of less than £8,500 a year.

Income tax: simplifying the administration of employee expenses, including preventing salary sacrifice

The administration of tax relief for employee expenses where the employer pays or reimburses them, or provides benefits-in-kind in respect of them, is being simplified. The new provisions will take effect from 6 April 2016.

Broadly, the measure removes the reporting requirement and the requirement for employers to apply to HMRC for a dispensation in order to pay qualifying expenses and benefits-in-kind. It also more closely aligns the tax rules to the existing National Insurance contributions (NICs) treatment of expenses payments.

The measure also prevents expenses being paid free of tax and NICs as part of a 'salary sacrifice' arrangement. These arrangements require the employee to give up a right to a part of their salary in exchange for the payment of those expenses, in order to reduce the NICs liabilities of both the employer and employee.

Income tax: statutory exemption for trivial benefits-in-kind

From 6 April 2015, a statutory exemption is being introduced, which will allow employers to identify and treat certain low value benefits-in-kind provided to employees as 'trivial'. Those benefits will become exempt from income tax and National Insurance contributions (NICs), and therefore not need to be reported to HMRC. A number of conditions will need to be satisfied for the exemption to apply and there will be an upper limit per individual benefit of £50.

There will be an annual cap of £300 for office holders of close companies, and employees who are family members of those office holders. Those affected by this cap will be able to receive a maximum of £300 worth of trivial benefits in kind each year exempt from tax and NICs.

Real time collection of tax on benefits-in-kind and expenses through voluntary payrolling

Changes are being made to the legislation to provide for voluntary payrolling of benefits-in-kind. Broadly, the changes mean that, from 2016/17, employers will have the option to payroll voluntary car, car fuel, medical insurance and subscriptions such as gym memberships. Employers opting to payroll benefits-in-kind will report the value of the benefits through real time information, and subsequently will not be required to report them on annual forms P11D.

Tax exemption for travel expenses of members of local authorities

Legislation in Finance Bill 2015 will exempt payment of councillors' travel expenses from a charge to tax and Class 1 National Insurance contributions (NICs). The exemption takes effect from 6 April 2015.

The exemption will include expenses paid for journeys between the councillor's home and most frequently used local authority office, except where the councillor's home is more than 20 miles from the boundary of the local authority area. However, the exemption will only apply where payments are made by a local authority under certain provisions set by Treasury regulations.

The current rules for mileage allowance payments (MAPs), approved mileage allowance payments (AMAPs), and mileage allowance relief (MAR) will continue to apply to business travel undertaken by a councillor in their own vehicle. Journeys between a councillor's home and most frequently used local authority office, where their home is either in the local authority area or within 20 miles of the boundary of the area, will be treated as business travel when calculating MAPs and applying the AMAPs limits, but will not be treated as business travel for calculating MAR.

Exemption from income tax for the bereavement support payment

Provisions for a new bereavement support payment are contained in the Pensions Act 2014 and will commence from a date to be set. Finance Bill 2015 will include provisions to ensure that once introduced, such payments will be exempt from income tax.

Exemption from income tax and National Insurance contributions: lump sums provided under armed forces early departure scheme

The current income tax exemption for lump sum payments under the armed forces early departure payment 2005 (EDP 05) scheme is to be extended from 1 April 2015 to include payments made under the new EDP 15 scheme. Such payments will also be exempt for National Insurance contributions purposes.

Income tax: gift aid intermediaries

Finance Bill 2105 introduces changes that will allow for gift aid declarations (GADs) to be made by intermediaries representing individuals on behalf of those individuals, and allow charities to use such GADs to claim gift aid. Broadly, this will be done by extending the meaning of 'qualifying donation' to include 'an intermediary representing the individual'. This change will take effect from the date that Finance Bill 2015 receives Royal Assent, with regulations setting out the detailed operating model(s) for non-charity intermediaries to be consulted upon and made thereafter.

Income tax and corporation tax: tax relief for businesses contributing to a partnership funding flood defence scheme

With effect from 1 January 2015, contributions of money or services made to a flood and coastal erosion risk management (FCERM) partnership funding scheme will be deductible from the profits of the business for corporation tax or income tax purposes.

Increase to remittance basis charge

The remittance basis charge, paid by non-UK domiciled individuals who have been resident in the UK for more than 12 of the past 14 years, and who wish to retain access to the remittance basis of taxation, is to rise from £50,000 to £60,000 with effect from 6 April 2015. Also from that date, a new charge of £90,000 will be introduced for people who have been resident in the UK for more than 17 of the past 20 years. The current £30,000 charge will remain the same for those who are resident in the UK for seven of the past nine years.

Investment managers: disguised fee income

Sums received by individuals involved in investment management for a private equity fund or other investment fund, who are members of a limited partnership or limited liability partnership, or involved in arrangements including partnerships, which are for investment management services will be charged to income tax and Class 4 National Insurance contributions.

The charge will apply regardless of how the sums are described and whatever the legal form of payment. The proposed change will not affect returns reflecting performance of investments under management, commonly known as carried interest, nor investments by managers known as co-investment. This change will have effect on all disguised fees arising on or after 6 April 2015, whenever the arrangements were entered into.

In order to reflect industry practice on performance related returns the charge on non-UK residents will be restricted to UK duties.

Income tax and capital gains tax: social investment tax relief – enlarging the scheme

The current limit on the amount that can be invested in a qualifying social enterprise for the purposes of social investment tax relief (SITR) (£275,000 over a three-year period) is being replaced with a new annual investment limit of £5 million, with an overall limit of £15 million on total investment. This change will take effect as soon as possible on or after 6 April 2015, but is subject to state aid clearance.

In addition, legislation contained in Finance Bill 2015 will permit secondary legislation to be made to amend the definition of excluded activities for the purposes of SITR. Subject to state aid clearance, secondary legislation will allow certain small agricultural and horticultural projects that will not be eligible for direct payments under the Common Agricultural Policy (CAP) reforms to be qualifying trades for the purposes of SITR. Broadly, land holdings of below:

- five hectares in England and Wales; and
- three hectares in Scotland and Northern Ireland

will no longer qualify for direct payment subsidies under the CAP but will become eligible for SITR.

Income tax and capital gains tax: changes to venture capital schemes for companies and community organisations benefiting from energy subsidies

The list of excluded activities within the tax-advantaged venture capital and social investment tax relief (SITR) schemes is to be amended. Companies (excluding community organisations) whose trade consists wholly or substantially of the subsidised generation of energy from renewable sources where anaerobic digestion or hydroelectric power is involved, or where a company enters into a contract for difference, will cease to be eligible for investment under the seed enterprise investment scheme (SEIS), enterprise investment scheme (EIS) and venture capital trust (VCT) scheme. Investments in companies receiving foreign subsidies similar to contracts for difference will also be excluded from such schemes.

When the enlargement of SITR receives state aid clearance, community energy companies whose trade consists wholly or substantially of the subsidised generation of energy from renewable sources, will cease to be eligible for investment under the SEIS, EIS and VCT schemes. At the same time, the qualifying activities under SITR will be amended to allow activities for

which a feed-in-tariff (FIT) subsidy is receivable. The measure will apply in respect of UK subsidies and overseas equivalents.

These changes are generally expected to take effect from 6 April 2015, but are subject to state aid clearance. (TIIN 10 December 2014)

Income tax: special purpose share schemes

Companies use special purpose share schemes (often called 'B share schemes') to offer shareholders the choice to receive either a dividend or to receive a similar amount through an issue of new shares that are subsequently purchased by the company or sold to a pre-arranged third party.

Finance Bill 2015 contains legislation designed to align the tax consequences of that choice to ensure that all shareholders are taxed as if they had received a dividend. The changes have effect for receipts on or after 6 April 2015.

Income tax: miscellaneous loss relief

Legislation included in Finance Bill 2015 will deny miscellaneous loss relief for income tax purposes where a loss arises as a result of 'relevant tax avoidance arrangements'. The legislation will also deny miscellaneous loss relief against miscellaneous income that arises as a result of 'relevant tax avoidance arrangements'. 'Relevant tax avoidance arrangements' are arrangements to which the person is party and the main purpose, or one of the main purposes, is to obtain a reduction in tax liability by means of loss relief under ITA 2007, s 152.

New legislation will also limit the miscellaneous income against which a miscellaneous loss can be deducted to miscellaneous income chargeable to income tax under, or by virtue of, the same provision as the loss would have been chargeable had it been profits or other income instead of a loss.

The changes denying loss relief where a miscellaneous loss, or miscellaneous income, arises as a result of relevant tax avoidance arrangements apply in relation to losses and income arising on and after 3 December 2014. The change limiting the deduction of miscellaneous losses to miscellaneous income of the same type will have effect for 2015/16 onwards.

Income tax: deduction at source from interest paid on private placements

A new exemption means that there will be no obligation to deduct income tax from yearly interest paid on private placements which meet certain conditions. Such instruments will be known as 'qualifying private placements'.

Finance Bill 2015 sets out the conditions, including requirements that the instrument must represent a loan relationship of a company, be issued for a minimum period of three years, and not be listed on a recognised stock exchange. In addition, the primary legislation will allow for further conditions to be set out in regulations, in relation to the security itself and the terms and conditions of its issuance, and in relation to the issuer and holder of the security. The changes are expected to apply from the date that Finance Bill 2015 receives Royal Assent.

Capital allowances: extension of enhanced capital allowances for car and goods vehicles to 2018

Capital expenditure on plant and machinery normally permits a claim to capital allowances at 18% a year on a reducing balance. Certain assets qualify for 100% capital allowances in the year of acquisition, and these enhanced capital allowances (ECAs) are currently available, amongst other assets, to cars emitting 95 grams or less of CO_2 per kilometre, as well as electrically propelled cars, zero-emission goods vehicles and equipment required to refuel natural gas, biogas and hydrogen powered vehicles. These enhanced capital allowances were due to end on 31 March 2015, but will be extended to 31 March 2018 for corporation tax payers and 5 April 2018 for income tax payers.

There will be a supplementary rule to prevent such claims, however, if another form of state aid is already being, or will be, received.

Capital allowances: anti-avoidance rules for plant and machinery

An announcement was made on 26 February 2015 that a loophole in the capital allowances anti-avoidance rules would be closed down with immediate effect. Where a person acquires plant or machinery for no consideration, no capital allowances are due as there is no qualifying expenditure. It appears that businesses have been 'refreshing' the capital allowances by transactions with related parties, involving sale and leaseback, sale and hire purchase or sale and long funding leases. As a result, although the assets are acquired for no consideration, substantial capital allowances became available.

The new rules will deny capital allowances where a person disposes of an asset without bringing into account a disposal value, or where a person that is or was connected with that first person has acquired the assets without capital expenditure. The new rules also apply in situations where there is deemed to be no expenditure.

The restriction will not apply if the person acquiring the asset has incurred 'qualifying revenue expenditure', being an arm's length price on revenue account, or is a manufacturer that incurred all the normal costs of manufacturing the assets. Nor will there be a restriction where the person disposing of the assets is deemed to have incurred expenditure, such as if assets have been gifted.

This loophole will be closed for all transactions taking place on or after 26 February 2015. Draft legislation was also published on that date.

It is perhaps interesting to note that the TIIN announcing this measure states that there is neither cost nor benefit to the Exchequer!

Pensions and National Insurance

Pensions

Defined contribution schemes

In his budget last year, the Chancellor announced significant changes to the tax treatment of defined contribution (DC) pensions. Following consultation, particularly on the implications for defined benefit (DB) schemes, the changes have now been enacted through the Taxation of Pensions Act 2014 ('the Act') which introduces the 'flexi-access drawdown fund'.

These changes have dominated the pensions industry over the last 12 months and, despite the proximity to 6 April 2015 when the raft of changes come into effect, there are many areas the industry needs to analyse and understand, not least the area of member 'advice'; last year's pledge to guarantee an offer of 'free, impartial, face-to-face advice' for all retiring on DC pensions has been replaced by free generic guidance through the 'pensions wise' service. The Chancellor announced in his budget an additional £1.95 million funding for pensions wise in the 2015/16 tax year.

Members of DC schemes will certainly have greater flexibility on how to take their pension fund benefits, but there is now a real concern over the risks this poses to many, including the risks of mis-selling, over-charging for flexibilities and the basic risk of members exhausting their pension pots before they die.

Extending death relaxation to annuities

As announced in Autumn Statement 2014, with effect from 6 April 2015 the future payments under certain joint life or guaranteed annuities will be able to continue to beneficiaries tax-free on a member's death before age 75, provided no payments have been made to the beneficiary before 6 April 2015. This was to mirror the freedoms extended on death where DC pension pots are not annuitised.

In view of changes since the Budget 2014 announcement, a new impact note was published alongside the Act, to cover the full extent of the freedoms in the Act.

Income tax exemption when employer pays for independent advice to employees

A new income tax exemption is to be included in Finance Bill 2015 to cover the specific situation where an employer carries out a 'transfer incentive exercise' and offers members of its defined benefit (DB) scheme the option to transfer to a DC scheme (usually coupled with some form of financial incentive to the member). The employer will be required to pay for members to receive independent financial advice from an approved adviser and the objective of the exemption is to avoid the member being taxed or charged National Insurance contri-butions (NICs) on the cost of that advice, as a benefit-in-kind, and to avoid the employer being charged NICs on the payment.

Creating a secondary annuity market

The Chancellor confirmed a policy proposed by the pensions minister some months ago relating to the creation of a secondary market for annuities, where individuals with an existing annuity can gain flexibility in their position by assigning their annuity to a third party. This will involve removing the 55% unauthorised payment tax charge that would current apply on assignment, and possibly involve other facilitating secondary legislation.

The government's intention is to give annuity holders similar pensions freedoms to those accorded to DC pension pot holders. In particular, it is hoped to offer annuitants the option to assign their annuity policy to a third party and have options of a lump sum cash payment, a 'flexi-access drawdown fund' (akin to the option available from 2015, for a DC pot holder) or a flexible annuity. A consultative document entitled 'Creating a secondary annuity market' has been published and issued by HM Treasury and the Department for Work and Pensions jointly, with a consultation running until 18 June 2015. The changes are intended to be effected from 6 April 2016.

Extension of pension flexibilities to QROPS

Following consultation over the extension of DC freedoms to qualifying recognised overseas pension schemes (QROPS), new regulations applying from 6 April 2015 are likely, despite the deferral of a new QROPS re-notification process from April 2015 until April 2016, to allow EU based QROPS to offer members similar freedoms to UK registered pension schemes, as long as new reporting requirements are met. However, non-EU jurisdictions may have to wait before the requirement to apply 70% of UK tax relieved monies to provide an income for life is dropped.

Pensions lifetime allowance and annual allowance

Following cuts in the annual allowance (AA) from £50,000 to £40,000, and in the lifetime allowance (LTA) from £1.5 million to £1.25 million, with effect from the 2014/15 tax year, whilst no further changes were announced in last year's Autumn Statement, the Chancellor has announced a reduction in the LTA to £1 million from the 2016/17 tax year, with a re-introduction of inflation (ie consumer price index) indexation of the LTA from April 2018. Annual indexation was an integral feature of the LTA regime introduced in 2006 and applied until 2010, when the LTA stood at £1.8 million. The Chancellor announced that he did not intend to reduce the AA.

National insurance contributions

Abolition of employer contributions for apprentices under 25

From April 2016, employers of apprentices under the age of 25 will no longer be required to pay secondary Class 1 (employer) National Insurance contributions on earnings up to the upper earnings limit for those employees.

Employment allowance extension to personal carers

The employment allowance, which allows employers to deduct up to £2,000 per annum from their secondary Class 1 NIC liability, is to be extended to individuals who employ care and support workers. This change applies from 6 April 2015.

Corporation tax and diverted profits tax

Corporation tax, etc

Bank loss relief restriction

A company's corporation tax profits are reduced by the set-off of brought forward trading losses, non-trading loan relationship deficits and management expenses. There is no restriction on the use of these losses, so businesses often pay no corporation tax until the losses have been exhausted.

There are significant losses in the banking sector, which are considered to be 'a consequence of banks' performance during the financial crisis and the costs associated with subsequent misconduct and mis-selling scandals' (see the TIIN announcing this measure). The Government's view is that it is not right that these entities should then pay no corporation tax while they use up the losses that have arisen through their own bad behaviour, so the use of losses by banks and building societies within the charge to UK corporation tax will be restricted to 50% of their profits each year. This restriction will apply from 1 April 2015 in respect of tax losses that have accrued prior to that date.

This will substantially increase the period over which such losses are relieved by the banks, and it is calculated that the beneficial result for the Treasury will be around £700 million a year extra tax for the years 2015/16 to 2019/20.

Following a period of consultation, the Government will be making a change to the measure's targeted anti-avoidance rule and introducing a £25 million allowance for affected building societies.

Bank levy

The bank levy will be increased to 0.21% from 1 April 2015, and the half rate will be increased to 0.105% from the same date. The previous increase was on 1 January 2014, to 0.156% and 0.078%, respectively.

The bank levy is to ensure that the banking sector makes a fair contribution and reflects the risks posed to the financial system and the wider economy by the sector. But this is to be balanced against general financial stability and the ability of the banks to lend, to assist businesses and hence general economic growth. An increased contribution is considered reasonable as banks' balance sheets strengthen and the banks are returning to profitability.

The Government has previously said that it expects the levy to raise at least £2.5 billion annually. The TIIN announcing this measure shows an increased contribution as a result of the rate rise of £685 million in 2015/16 and £925 million a year thereafter.

Simplifying link company requirements for consortium claims

Corporation tax group relief can be transferred from consortium companies to groups which own shares in that consortium.

However, a requirement for that relief is that the 'link company', ie the company which is both a member of the group and of the consortium, must satisfy specific residence requirements. It must either be located in the UK or, if located in the European Economic Area, it must also satisfy other conditions.

For accounting periods ending on or after 10 December 2014, all requirements relating to the location of the link company are removed.

This is stated to be a simplification of the tax system, which of course it is. What HMRC's announcement of this measure fails to mention is that this is a response forced on the Government by its defeat in the Court of Justice of the European Union in the case of *Felixstowe Dock and Railway Co Ltd*.

Accelerated payments and group relief

The accelerated payment regime has been very highly publicised since its inception in Finance Act 2014 and, indeed, during the consultation periods over the new legislation prior to its enactment. In essence, if tax is in dispute in respect of certain types of tax avoidance scheme (largely, those which have been reported under the disclosure of tax avoidance schemes rules, or to which the general anti-abuse rule (GAAR) applies), HMRC can issue an accelerated payment notice (APN) requiring the relevant taxpayers to pay to HMRC the tax currently in dispute.

There are two reasons for this: the main reason is a view that the Exchequer should not be deprived of tax receipts for the many years it often takes to ascertain whether the tax avoidance schemes are effective. Given that HMRC has publicised heavily the fact that it has won some 80% of the cases it has taken to the tribunals and courts in respect of tax avoidance schemes, HMRC's view is that most of the money collected under APNs will not have to be repaid. The secondary point is that a reasonable proportion of the people who have implemented tax avoidance schemes might, by the time the scheme is eventually defeated in the courts, be unable to pay the tax, either through having spent the money or through having died or become insolvent. It is, of course, unlikely that the Government will become insolvent and be unable to repay any

tax that it is required to repay in respect of schemes that turn out to be successful.

Where groups of companies are involved in tax planning, a company might generate a loss by the use of a tax avoidance scheme and surrender that loss to another group company; so the other group company has got the ultimate tax advantage, but the APN can only be issued to the company that implemented the scheme.

To prevent further abuse in this area, there will be a new rule that prevents the group relief surrender being made while the relevant tax is in dispute. In effect, rather than being an APN in the generally understood way, this will mean that the company that would have claimed the group relief will simply have to pay the corporation tax without any group relief until the dispute is settled.

This new rule will take effect from the date of Royal Assent to Finance Bill 2015.

Restricting relief for internally-generated goodwill transfers between related parties on incorporation

On incorporation of a business, any goodwill transferred into the company should appear on the balance sheet at market value, as acquired goodwill on a business acquisition. The amortisation or impairment of that goodwill is generally allowable for tax purposes under the accounts-based tax rules for corporate intangibles in CTA 2009, Pt 8. This advantage is being removed in respect of transfers of intangible assets to connected companies on or after 3 December 2014, unless a contract for the transfer had become unconditional before that date. The change is obviously linked to the restriction of entrepreneurs' relief on incorporation.

Where goodwill or similar assets are acquired by a company from an individual who is a related party in relation to the company, or from a partnership where at least one member is a related party in relation to the company, the new rules will deny any deductions for amortisation or impairment of the goodwill; and any debit arising on realisation of goodwill will be treated as a non-trading debit. So if the goodwill is realised at a loss, the debit appears to be allowable for corporation tax purposes, but as a non-trading debit, which can only be used against the company's other profits of the period, or carried forward.

These rules apply to 'relevant assets', meaning goodwill, customer information, customer relationships, unregistered trademarks or other signs, as well as licences in respect of any such assets, relating to the business or part of the business that is transferred to the company. So the legislation does not just apply to goodwill (although it will be the most common case) but also to these other assets which are considered, by HMRC at least, to be closely related to the goodwill. For example, an unregistered trademark is considered part of the goodwill of a business, as highlighted in *Iliffe News & Media Ltd* [2012] UKFTT 696 (TC).

Goodwill transferred on incorporation could have been acquired in previous arm's length transactions. In such cases, some deductions are allowed in the company for amortisation, etc, by applying a factor, the appropriate multiplier (AM) to the deduction in the profit and loss account. AM is a fraction whose numerator is the 'notional accounting value' of the goodwill, as if GAAP-compliant accounts had been drawn up by the transferor immediately prior to transfer of the business to the company, on the assumption that the business was a going concern. The denominator is the total goodwill recognised by the company, whether capitalised or recognised in determining profit and loss. This is not a favourable calculation, as the notional accounting value will usually be the amortised cost of the goodwill arising on previous third-party business acquisitions, whereas the capitalised expenditure in the company's accounts might well be substantially greater. So any enhancement to previously acquired goodwill prior to incorporation is not recognised by this calculation.

On realisation, any debit is multiplied by AM, again, to determine the proportion that should be treated as a non-trade debit. The rest, relating to goodwill originally acquired from third parties, is treated normally.

In the Autumn Statement 2014 document, the change is described (at para 2.146) as being to 'restrict unfair tax advantages on incorporation' and is listed under the main heading of 'Avoidance and evasion'! A more honest approach would be to say openly that this generous tax treatment on incorporation can no longer be afforded, although it is also noted that that the anticipated yield is relatively low, being £5 million in 2014/15, rising to £155 million in 2019/20. The figures given are identical to those given in the TIIN announcing the restriction of entrepreneurs' relief on incorporation.

Modernising the taxation of corporate debt and derivative contracts

Since the introduction of the current rules for loan relationships in 2006, there have been substantial developments in both business practice and accounting, including, for example, the introduction of FRS 102 from 1 January 2015. To take account of these changes, and also to simplify the rules generally, a number of changes are provided for in Finance Bill 2015. The package was originally announced at Budget 2013 followed by a consultation from June of that year and the Government's response published on 10 December 2013. A technical note outlining the proposed changes was published on 8 April 2014.

Two changes come into force during 2015:

- There are currently rules allowing debt to be swapped in consideration of the issue of equity, potentially of a substantially lower nominal amount, to assist companies in restructuring. These rules will be extended so that where the debts of a financially distressed company are being restructured so the company can remain solvent, credits arising will not be taxable. This is intended to cover situations where there is a release or modification of the debt generating what would otherwise be taxable credits. The new provisions apply to releases or modifications on or after 1 January 2015.
- A new general anti-avoidance rule for the loan relationships and derivative contracts regimes will be introduced, allowing the repeal of a number of existing specific anti-avoidance rules. The new rules will deny the benefit of arrangements entered into 'with a main purpose of obtaining a tax advantage by way of the loan relationships or derivative contracts rules', and will apply in respect of arrangements entered into on or after 1 April 2015.

Further proposed revisions in Finance Act 2015 will have effect in respect of company accounting periods commencing on or after 1 January 2016. These are:

- The current rules largely follow the accountancy treatment and this linkage between accountancy and tax will be 'clarified and strengthened'. The rules currently state that the amounts brought into account for tax 'must fairly represent' profits, gains and losses arising, but this requirement will be removed.
- The rules will be amended so that tax is based only on amounts shown as producing profits or losses for accounting purposes, broadly through the profit and loss account. Currently, gains or losses shown in equity or other reserves can also be taxable or relievable. There will be transitional rules to ensure that this measure is tax neutral.
- During 2015 there will be secondary legislation to update the rules on forex hedging, convertible instruments and property based derivatives.
- Secondary legislation will be amended to facilitate the transaction to new accounting standards.

Preventing abuse of late paid interest rules

This measure also arises from the consultation on modifying the loan relationships rules. Generally, a debit is granted for interest on a loan relationship, or deep discounted security is granted for tax purposes, when the interest accrues. In certain cases, involving connected creditors in certain overseas territories (tax havens), the relief is restricted where the interest remains unpaid for at least 12 months, with a deduction only being granted when the interest is eventually paid.

The anti-avoidance impact of this rule was restricted in 2009 only to interest payable to connected tax haven companies, as a result of which its application is very narrow. Furthermore, it is understood that some companies are able to use these rules to obtain a more advantageous group relief position than was intended by the group relief rules. As a result, the Government has decided to repeal these rules in respect of new loans entered into on or after 3 December 2014. The Exchequer effect is considered to be negligible.

Where loans were entered into before 3 December 2014 the current rules in respect of the interest will apply until 31 December 2015, with the new rules applying from 1 January 2016, unless "material changes" are made to the loan in the transitional period, in which case the new rules will apply from the date of those changes.

Corporation tax: loss refresh prevention

Company losses can arise in a variety of categories, such as trading losses, excess management expenses, property business losses, etc. The use of these is relatively versatile in the year in which they arise, as they are usually available to set off against other profits that the company has that year, or to be surrendered to other group companies as group relief. But losses, etc that cannot be used that way are usually carried forward and their use in future accounting periods tends to be restricted to being set off against the profits of the business stream they arose in, and in the same company.

Companies have, therefore, used various methods to enhance the profits of the relevant business stream in order to use those losses, in a way that may generate other losses in the same year that can be used more flexibly. For example, a company with non-trading losses of some sort might be able to shelter rents that are paid to it by a trading company in the group, using the non-trading losses and generating trading losses (or smaller profits) in the trading company.

From Budget Day, 18 March 2015, there will be an anti-avoidance rule applying to trading losses, non-trading loan relationship debits, carried forward management expenses, including qualifying charitable donations treated as management expenses and management expenses arising on cessation of a property business. If there are arrangements to use those losses, it is reasonable to suppose that they could only have been used because of the arrangements, the company or a connected company then has a deductible amount (ie the 'refreshed' loss) and the main or one of the main purposes of the arrangements is the tax advantage so accruing, then the use of the existing losses will be denied. So the artificially generated profits will remain in charge and the new losses will be available, as (it is thought) will the old losses, if they are used for a legitimate purpose.

The TIIN announcing this measure states that this should not impact on genuine commercial transactions, although it also states that HMRC will apply the new rules if the tax benefit is greater than the expected economic advantage, which is bound to lead to substantial uncertainty, especially as there is no formal clearance facility (although HMRC's business 'customers' may be able to use the non-statutory business clearance facility).

Oil and gas taxation: investment allowance

For investment expenditure incurred on or after 1 April 2015, a new investment allowance equal to 62.5% of a company's investment expenditure will reduce the amount of adjusted ring fence profits subject to the supplementary charge.

Oil and gas taxation: reduction in petroleum revenue tax

The rate of petroleum revenue tax (PRT) payable in respect of profits from oil and gas production is reduced from 50% to 35%, with effect for all chargeable periods ending after 31 December 2015.

Oil and gas taxation: reduction in supplementary charge

With effect from 1 January 2015 and subject to transitional provisions, the rate of supplementary charge payable in respect of profits from oil and gas production in the UK and UK Continental Shelf is reduced from 32% to 20%.

Oil and gas taxation: high pressure high temperature cluster area allowance

To encourage the development of high pressure high temperature (HPHT) oil and gas projects, capital expenditure incurred on cluster area oil and gas projects on or after 3 December 2014 can qualify for a new HPHT cluster area allowance to reduce the amount of adjusted ring fence profits subject to the supplementary charge.

Following consultation, the legislation has been revised to introduce a power to extend the definition of qualifying expenditure in the future by secondary legislation, and to introduce a restriction for expenditure incurred on the acquisition of a licence interest.

Oil and gas taxation: extension of ring fence expenditure supplement

The ring fence expenditure supplement has allowed companies involved in the exploration, appraisal and development of oil and gas to claim a 10% per annum uplift to qualifying pre-commencement expenditure and losses for up to six accounting periods, and this was extended last year to ten accounting periods for onshore activities.

It is now extended to ten accounting periods for offshore activities, effective for pre-trading expenditure and losses of accounting periods ending on or after 5 December 2013. Claims in respect of extended ring fence expenditure supplement no longer apply.

Research and development tax credits: increasing generosity

For qualifying expenditure incurred on or after 1 April 2015, the rate of the 'above the line' expenditure credit for large company research and development (R&D) activity is increased from 10% to 11%; this remains an optional alternative to the 130% enhanced deduction available to large companies. From the same date, the enhanced deduction available to small and medium enterprises (SMEs) is increased from 225% to 230%.

Research and development tax credits: consumables

From 1 April 2015, new rules restrict the expenditure on consumable items that qualifies for R&D relief under any of the existing schemes, ie the enhanced deduction for SMEs, the enhanced deduction for large companies and the alternative 'above the line' expenditure credit for large companies.

Where the R&D activity results in goods or services sold in the normal course of a company's business, the cost of consumable items reflected in those goods or services will not attract tax relief. Qualifying expenditure on consumable items will be limited to the cost of items fully used up in the R&D activity itself.

Following consultation, the restriction will not apply where the product of the R&D is transferred as waste, or where it is transferred but no consideration is received.

Creative tax reliefs: increasing the rate of film tax relief

Changes will be made to film tax relief with effect from 1 April 2015 or, if later, from the date the changes receive state aid approval. The distinction between limited budget films and all others will be removed, and the rate of tax relief is to be 25% for all qualifying core expenditure, for all eligible film productions.

Creative tax reliefs: high-end television tax relief

Subject to state aid approval, the rules for television tax relief are to be changed for qualifying expenditure incurred on or after 1 April 2015. The minimum UK expenditure requirement for high-end television or animation will be cut from 25% to 10%, and the cultural test will be modernised.

Creative tax reliefs: children's television tax relief

To encourage the production of culturally British children's television programmes in the UK, the pre-existing television tax reliefs for animation and high-end TV are extended to children's programming where expenditure is incurred on or after 1 April 2015. Relief applies at 25% on enhanceable expenditure for all eligible children's TV programmes. Children's programming is not subject to the £1 million per programme hour threshold or the 30-minute slot length that apply to high-end TV programmes.

The relief allows eligible companies to claim an additional deduction in computing their taxable profits, and where that additional deduction results in a loss to surrender those losses for a payable tax credit.

Following consultation, this new relief has been extended to children's games shows and competitions.

Diverted profits tax

Diverted profits tax

A new tax, the diverted profits tax (DPT), aims to counter the use of aggressive tax planning by multinationals to divert profits from the UK, and is to apply at a rate of 25% from 1 April 2015.

DPT is aimed at large enterprises. It targets arrangements which avoid a UK permanent establishment, and comes into effect if a person is carrying on activity in the UK in connection with supplies of goods and services by a non-UK resident company to customers in the UK. It also seeks to prevent companies with an existing UK taxable presence from creating tax advantages by using transactions or entities that lack economic substance. The tax is only payable following a notice issued by HMRC, but once such a notice is issued it must be paid within 30 days.

HMRC's draft guidance on DPT is at www.gov.uk/government/publications/diverted-profits-tax-guidance.

Following consultation, changes have been made to clarify certain aspects of the new regime.

Property tax, indirect tax, customs duties, etc

Value added tax (VAT)

VAT registration thresholds

From 1 April 2015, the VAT registration threshold will be increased from £81,000 to £82,000, and the de-registration threshold from £79,000 to £80,000.

Deductions relating to foreign branches

This measure will result in an amendment to the VAT Regulations 1995 (SI 1995/2518), and will mean that supplies made by foreign branches can no longer be taken into account when calculating how much VAT incurred on overhead costs can be deducted by partly exempt businesses in the UK.

The measure will simplify the tax system and make it fairer by mitigating the risk that some partly exempt businesses could artificially increase the amount of input tax that they are entitled to deduct. It also implements a 2013 decision of the Court of Justice of the European Union (*Credit Lyonnais*).

Refunds for palliative care charities

This measure will come into force on 1 April 2015, and will introduce a new VAT refund scheme for palliative care charities. It will enable these charities to reclaim the VAT they incur on purchases made to support their non-business activities.

Summary of Budget Proposals 18 March 2015

Legislation will be introduced in Finance Bill 2015 to add new sections 33C and 33D to the Value Added Tax Act 1994, which will allow palliative care charities to claim a refund of VAT incurred for the purpose of their non-business activities. The legislation will define palliative care charities. The term 'charity' will take its meaning from Finance Act 2010, Sch 6.

Power to provide for refunds to certain persons

This measure will create a new Value Added Tax Act (VATA) 1994, s 33E, which will provide refunds to named non-departmental public bodies, and similar public bodies, of the VAT incurred as a part of shared services arrangements used to support their non-business activities. Ordinarily, VAT can only be recovered on purchases made to support a person's taxable business activities.

The measure will ensure that what would otherwise be irrecoverable VAT does not deter public bodies from sharing back-office services, where this would otherwise result in greater efficiencies of scale.

It will have effect from the date of Royal Assent to Finance Bill 2015.

Refunds of VAT to search and rescue charities

This measure will provide for refunds of VAT incurred on the purchase of goods and services, and the acquisition and importation of goods from outside the UK to search and rescue charities (ie charities whose main purpose is to support, develop and promote the activities of charities established to search for and rescue people, and air ambulance charities) used for their non-business activities. Ordinarily VAT can only be recovered on purchases made for taxable business activities.

The measure will give search and rescue charities broadly the same level of VAT recovery as is presently afforded to the established emergency services.

It will have effect from 1 April 2015.

Refunds to strategic highways companies

This measure will provide for VAT refunds to the strategic highways company on certain services which it outsources.

This is to ensure that irrecoverable VAT does not act as a barrier to the outsourcing of services from the public sector to the private sector where this would result in efficiencies of scale. Government departments can reclaim the VAT incurred on certain services which they and their executive agencies have outsourced. The Highways Agency is an executive agency of the Department for Transport and thus the VAT it incurs on the purchase of any listed services is included in the Department for Transport's claim.

On 1 April 2015, the activities of the Highways Agency will be transferred to a strategic highways company. Since this company will not be an executive agency of the Department for Transport, and since it too will not be engaged in any substantial business activities, the existing legislation will not permit it to recover VAT. This measure will amend UK legislation to enable the new company to recover VAT, just as the Highways Agency does via the Department for Transport.

The measure will have effect on and after 1 April 2015.

Refunds of non-recoverable VAT for the London Legacy Development Corporation

This measure will specify the London Legacy Development Corporation (LLDC) as a body to which VATA 1994, s 33 applies. This will entitle the LLDC to refunds of VAT in respect of their non-business activities.

The Government's objective is that irrecoverable VAT should not be a cost borne from local taxation. This is achieved by refunding to named bodies the VAT they incur on purchases made to support their non-business activities.

During the bid to host the Olympic and Paralympics Games, promises were made to redevelop the Olympic Park after the games had finished. The promise was to provide social, economic and environmental benefits for local communities. The Olympic Park is in a Mayoral Development Area and the LLDC was established under the Localism Act 2011 for the purpose of providing this sustainable legacy. The Government wants to ensure that the associated VAT incurred in the redevelopment of the Olympic Park is refunded.

The statutory instrument will have effect from 1 April 2015.

Refunds to medical courier charities

Legislation will be introduced in Finance Bill 2015 to add new sections 33C and 33D to VATA 1994 to include a new VAT refund scheme for blood bike charities to recover VAT on the purchase of goods and services relating to their non-business activities.

Excise duty

Air passenger duty

Currently, children under two years old are exempt from air passenger duty (APD). This staggered measure extends the exemption to children under 12 (with effect from 1 May 2015) and subsequently to children under 16 (with effect from 1 March 2016), provided they are travelling in economy class or equivalent.

APD rates will increase by the retail price index (RPI) from 1 April 2016.

Alcohol duty – registration of wholesalers

This significant measure introduces a registration scheme for alcohol wholesalers, ie those selling alcoholic drinks to another business. This registration will only be granted to those who can demonstrate to HMRC that they are 'fit and proper' businesses. Additionally, those buying alcohol for retail or further wholesale supply will be required to buy from registered businesses. This is an attempt to stem the trade in alcoholic drinks where excise duty has not been paid or accounted for by limiting legal transactions to those who can prove compliance. Wholesalers must apply between October 2015 and the end of that year.

Following a period of assurance checking of applicants' businesses, the measure will come fully into effect from 1 April 2017.

Alcohol duty – rates

From 23 March 2015, the duty rates on general beer, sprits and lower strength cider will be reduced by 2%. The duty rate on low-strength beer will be reduced by 6% and the total duty rate on high-strength beer will be reduced by 0.75%. The duty rate on high-strength still cider will be reduced by 1.3% and the duty rates on wine below 22% abv and high-strength sparkling cider will be frozen.

Tobacco duty – anti-forestalling

Forestalling is the process where producers clear large quantities of tobacco in advance of a budget, paying duty at the current rate in order to avoid the increase in duty on the product. This measure will prevent manufacturers from pursuing this practice for three months before a budget. It will commence in time to apply to Budget 2016.

Tobacco duty – rates

Duty rates on tobacco products will increase by 2% above the RPI. These changes will come into effect from 6pm on 18 March 2015.

Fuel duty

Aqua methanol is an alternative engine fuel, which is seen as less harmful to the environment. To further encourage its use, fuel duty on aqua methanol will be applied at a reduced rate from 1 April 2015.

The Government will cancel the RPI inflation fuel duty increase of 0.54 pence per litre scheduled for 1 September 2015.

Rural fuel rebate scheme extension

The Council of the European Union has fully approved the Government's application to extend the rural fuel duty rebate scheme to 17 areas of the UK mainland. The scheme will be implemented on 1 April 2015, and will enable retailers in eligible areas to register for a five pence per litre fuel duty discount.

Summary of Budget Proposals 18 March 2015

Aggregates levy

Those who paid full rate aggregates levy on EU-sourced aggregate commercially exploited in Northern Ireland between 2004 and 2010 will be entitled to a refund of 80% to be paid as a credit against future liability. This measure follows a European Commission investigation into an earlier proposed rebate. It will take effect from the date of Royal Assent to Finance Bill 2015.

Landfill tax

From 1 April 2015, a new objective testing regime – based on an established scientific test – will be applied to the identification of landfill tax liability.

The standard and lower rates of landfill tax will increase in line with the RPI rounded to the nearest five pence from April 2016.

Carbon price floor

Fossil fuels used in a combined heat and power (CHP) plant – which efficiently uses fuel to produce both electricity and usable heat – will be exempted from the carbon price floor with effect from 1 April 2015, for plants using the fuels to produce good quality electricity. This will provide plants operating qualifying processes with a competitive advantage by effectively reducing the climate change levy on such fuels.

Gaming duty bands

The government will increase gaming duty bands in line with the RPI for accounting periods starting on or after 1 April 2015.

Climate change levy

The climate change levy main rates will increase in line with the RPI from 1 April 2016.

Stamp Taxes, CGT, ATED, IHT

Stamp taxes

Stamp duty land tax: reform of structure, rates and threshold

Following years of lobbying, the manner in which stamp duty land tax (SDLT) is calculated for residential property has undergone a radical change. This change takes effect from 4 December 2014 for purchases with an effective date thereafter. There are transitional provisions for purchases where there was an exchange of contracts before midnight on 3 December 2014 and completion some time later. The purchaser can choose whether to apply the new or old rates.

Under the old rules, if the purchase price for the property fell within a rate 'band', this would determine the rate of SDLT, which was applied to the entire consideration (ie the so-called 'slab' method). The new rules adopt a 'slice' methodology, whereby different parts of the price attract different rates of tax.

The new rates and thresholds are:

Property value band	Rate
£0–£125,000	0%
£125,001–£250,000	2%
£250,001–£925,000	5%
£925,001–£1,5 00,000	10%
£1,500,001+	12%

Very broadly, the effect is that less tax will be due on less expensive properties, whereas more will be due on more expensive properties.

There are no changes in respect of non-residential and mixed property transactions or on the net present value of rent.

Stamp duty land tax: alternative property finance

Currently, there is a stamp duty land tax (SDLT) relief for certain types of alternative property finance, originally intended to create a level playing field between Shariah compliant finance products and conventional mortgage finance. This is required since Shariah compliant finance often involves additional stages to the property purchase, which would otherwise result in additional tax.

This measure is intended to enable users of home purchase plans to benefit from those reliefs. Home purchase plans are another form of Shariah compliant finance, and as such are a way of financing a home purchase that does not involve the payment of interest. They are regulated in a similar way to conventional mortgages.

The measure will have effect for transactions with an effective date on or after the date on which Finance Bill 2015 receives Royal Assent.

Stamp duty land tax: treatment of shared ownership properties in lease and leaseback arrangements

This measure will extend the scope of stamp duty land tax (SDLT) multiple dwellings relief so that purchases from housing associations of superior leasehold interests in property subject to shared ownership leases can attract relief, where the transaction is part of a 'lease and leaseback' arrangement. This will reduce the SDLT cost to investors participating in funding arrangements of this kind.

Multiple dwellings relief works to reduce the rate of tax applicable to a transaction involving more than one dwelling to a minimum of 1%.

Legislation will be introduced in Finance Bill 2015 to extend multiple dwellings relief for the grant of a superior leasehold interest where: (a) the vendor is a 'qualifying body' for the purposes of the SDLT shared ownership legislation (typically a registered social landlord); (b) the transaction is part of the 'lease' element of a 'lease and leaseback' arrangement; and (c) the 'leaseback' element is eligible for relief.

This measure will have effect for transactions with an effective date on or after Royal Assent of Finance Bill 2015.

Capital gains tax and annual tax on enveloped dwellings

Capital gains tax: allowing entrepreneurs' relief on deferred gains

This is a measure intended to encourage further investment through the enterprise investment scheme (EIS) or through claims for social investment tax relief (SITR). Capital gains can be deferred into investments which qualify for EIS or SITR but, hitherto, if those reinvestments were subsequently sold, the capital gains tax charge on the deferred gain upon disposal of the EIS shares or the SITR investment would be at the normal rate for capital gains (18% or 28%). Under the new rules, if the deferred gain would have qualified for entrepreneurs' relief (ie the favourable 10% rate of capital gains tax) at the time of the original disposal, then the deferred gain will also qualify for entrepreneurs' relief on a subsequent disposal of the reinvestment.

This is a welcome change, which makes a great deal of sense. Clearly, if a gain was chargeable at 10%, it was unlikely that a taxpayer would wish to defer that gain by reinvestment, if the eventual gain were then to be chargeable at 28%. This is not a particularly expensive change as the costs are expected to be negligible for the next two years and no more than £5 million a year between 2016/17 and 2019/20.

The new rules apply in respect of assets disposals qualifying for entrepreneurs' relief on or after 3 December 2014, the date that the change was announced.

Capital gains tax: non-UK residents and UK residential property

This was a measure announced at Autumn Statement 2013. A consultation ran between March and June of that year, with a summary of responses published on 27 November 2014. Essentially, the measure is designed to extend the capital gains tax charge to disposals of UK residential property by certain persons who do not currently pay UK capital gains tax. In particular, individuals who are not resident in the UK do not currently pay capital gains tax on the disposal of UK residential property. And, while UK resident companies, or companies carrying on a trade in the UK through a permanent establishment, pay corporation tax on chargeable gains, this is at a favourable rate of 20% for all companies (from 1 April 2015) compared to capital gains tax rates of 28%.

The new rules will bring non-UK residents into the charge to capital gains tax when they dispose of a UK residential property interest. A residential property interest will include an interest in land that has consisted of or included a dwelling at any time during the period of ownership by that person, and the definition of dwelling will generally be based on that for the annual tax on enveloped dwellings (ATED). However, this will be modified in the context of provision of student accommodation to exclude purpose-built student accommodation that is not linked to a specific institution.

The private residence relief may still be available to non-UK resident individuals or trustees, although they will have to meet new qualifying conditions. But the relief will be restricted in respect of properties in a territory where the individual concerned is not tax resident and does not spend a minimum of 90 midnights in the property over the year.

There will also be an exemption for non-resident institutional investors with diverse ownership, and also for companies controlled by five or fewer persons. Where companies are within the new charge, but are part of a group, the assets of the group can be dealt with on a pooled basis, so that gains or losses of different group members that are not UK-resident can be offset in a year and unrelieved losses can be carried forward. Transfers within such a group will also be on a tax neutral basis.

The tax charge must be paid within 30 days of properties being conveyed, unless the person is already registered for self-assessment with HMRC, in which case the normal due date for capital gains tax would apply. The new rules will apply from 6 April 2015.

Capital gains tax: denying entrepreneurs' relief for disposals of goodwill to related companies

If an individual sells a business to a company, and the business is a trade, they would have expected to be able to claim entrepreneurs' relief and pay 10% capital gains tax on the disposal.

However, to the extent that the asset transferred is goodwill, entrepreneur's relief will no longer be available for disposals on or after 3 December 2014, under new TCGA 1992, s 169LA.

Where there is a qualifying business disposal involving the transfer of a business directly or indirectly to a close company, and the transferor is a related party in relation to the company, the goodwill will not be a relevant business asset for entrepreneurs' relief purposes, so the 10% CGT rate will not be available. In practice, this means that it is unlikely that businesses with substantial goodwill will be incorporated using this method, and people will revert to using the incorporation relief at TCGA 1992, s 162, or the gift relief at TCGA 1992, s 165.

Whether a person is a 'related party' in relation to a company is defined by the corporation tax rules for intangible fixed assets, in CTA 2009, Pt 8. The relevant rule in most cases will be that a participator in a close company is a related party in relation to that company (CTA 2009, s 835(5)). And the definition of close company includes non-UK resident companies that would be close if they were UK resident.

The main advantage of selling a business to a company is that this leaves a debt due to the transferor, which allows tax-efficient profit extraction from the company as the debt is repaid. HMRC's view is that such sums should be extracted from the company by more 'normal' means, such as dividends or salaries, so this provision 'removes an unfair advantage' (see the TIIN announcing this measure) and 'supports the government's objective to have a fair tax system' (see the explanatory notes to the draft legislation).

Following consultation, it was announced on 18 March 2015 that entrepreneurs' relief would continue to be available where the vendor does not hold or acquire any stake in the acquiring company. This allows exiting or retiring members of a partnership to claim entrepreneurs' relief in the normal way.

Capital gains tax: restricting entrepreneurs' relief on associated disposals

Under the entrepreneurs' relief rules, if a person makes a qualifying disposal of shares in a trading company or of assets of a trading partnership, further relief could be claimed on the 'associated disposal' of personal assets used in the trade. This facility was clearly being abused, with trivial disposal of business assets being used to 'frank' disposals of personal assets. To prevent this abuse, the associated disposal rules will only apply if the disposal of business assets involves at least 5% of the shares of the trading company or 5% of the assets of the partnership. This will apply to disposals on or after 18 March 2015.

Capital gains tax: entrepreneurs' relief, joint ventures and partnerships

Entrepreneurs' relief is intended to be available to people who have at least a 5% voting stake in a trading company. Where this is not the case, various joint venture and partnership structures have been used (or abused, in HMRC's view) to make entrepreneurs' relief available to individuals whose real stake in the underlying trade is less than 5%, often significantly so. Finance Bill 2015 will contain amendments to the definition of a 'trading company or a holding company of a trading group' to prevent this abuse in respect of all disposals on or after 18 March 2015.

Capital gains tax: exemption for certain wasting assets

Certain wasting assets are exempt from capital gains tax or corporation tax on gains, such as assets on which capital allowances can be claimed (ie even if they have not been claimed). HMRC recently lost a case where the exemption was claimed by a person who had not used the asset in their trade, but had loaned it to another person who used it as plant in their trade.

To prevent other persons setting up similar arrangements, the legislation (at TCGA 1992, s 45) will be amended so that the exemption for plant and machinery applies only where it has been used in the trade of the person making the disposal. This will apply to gains accruing from 1 April 2015 for corporation tax payers, and from 6 April 2015 for capital gains tax payers.

Annual tax on enveloped dwellings: increased charges

The annual charges for the annual tax on enveloped dwellings (ATED) will be increased by 50% above inflation as measured by the consumer prices index, so that the new charges are:

Property value	Annual charge in 2015–16
£2 million–£5 million	£23,350
£5 million–£10 million	£54,450
£10 million–£20 million	£109,050
£20 million+	£218,200

The new charges will apply from 1 April 2015.

Annual tax on enveloped dwellings

Currently non-natural persons (companies, partnerships with company members, and collective investment schemes) who own UK residential property within the thresholds for the annual tax on enveloped dwellings (ATED) charge must file detailed annual returns, even when there is no tax to pay due to a relief.

Measures to ease the administrative burden will have effect for the chargeable period 1 April 2015 to 31 March 2016 and thereafter. For chargeable persons who hold properties eligible for a relief from ATED, for the 2015/16 year only, returns must be filed by 1 October. For subsequent years the normal filing date of 30 April will apply.

Going forward, there will be a new type of ATED return (a 'relief declaration return'), for those persons holding properties eligible for a relief from ATED. For each type of relief being claimed a relief declaration return must be filed in respect of one or more properties held for that chargeable period. No details will be required of the individual properties eligible for that relief, although separate returns will be required where properties are acquired during the year that qualify for a different type of relief.

Capital gains tax: changes to the threshold amount for ATED-related CGT

From 6 April 2015, the sale of a property valued at a threshold amount of £1,000,000 will be subject to 'ATED-related CGT' where the annual tax on enveloped dwellings (ATED) has been paid on the property.

Summary of Budget Proposals 18 March 2015

This continues the Government's policy that certain UK residential property held by non-natural persons (companies, partnerships with company members and managers of collective investment schemes), which is subject to the ATED charge, will also be subject to capital gains tax (CGT) on its disposal.

There are exceptions from the charge, broadly, for property forming part of a genuine commercial activity, or used to house employees of that activity.

Budget 2014 announced two new bands for ATED to bring properties worth between £500,000 and £2 million into the charge. The threshold amount for consideration received will fall from £2 million to £1 million for disposals on or after 6 April 2015, and then to £500,000 for disposals on or after 6 April 2016.

The principle will be preserved that only the increase in a property's value during a period when it is liable to ATED is charged to ATED-related CGT. The current rate of ATED-related CGT is 28%, as opposed to 20% for most UK companies.

Inheritance tax

Simplifying charges on trusts and new rules to target avoidance through the use of multiple trusts

The calculation of trust charges is to be simplified by removing the need to include non-relevant property in the calculation. Broadly, this change will apply to all charges arising on or after 6 April 2015 in respect of relevant property trusts created on or after 10 December 2014, but it will also apply to relevant property trusts created before 10 December 2014 where there are additions made to more than one trust on the same day. The new rules which ignore non-relevant property in the calculation of the rate of charge on a 10-year anniversary will apply to all charges arising on or after 6 April 2015, regardless of when the trust was created.

In order to protect inheritance tax (IHT) revenues from avoidance by using multiple trusts, Finance Bill 2015 also contains changes regarding the addition of property to trusts on the same day. Where property is added to two or more settlements on the same day and after the commencement of those settlements, the value of the added property together with the value of property settled at the date of commencement (that is not already in a related settlement) will be brought into account in calculating the rate of tax for the purposes of ten year charges; for exit charges before the first 10-year anniversary; for exit charges between anniversaries; and for the charge on 18/25 trusts. The changes to existing trusts will not apply to a will executed before 10 December 2014, but this exclusion will be limited to deaths before 6 April 2016. This will allow a period of time for those affected to change their will and avoid unwanted tax consequences.

Claims for conditional exemption

From the date that Finance Bill 2015 receives Royal Assent, the requirement that a claim must be made and the property designated before the 10-year charge is being removed, and instead trustees will be allowed to make a claim for exemption within two years of the 10-year charge arising.

Pre-2006 settlements

With regard to settlements created by individuals before March 2006 giving themselves an interest in possession or to their spouse/widow/civil partner/surviving civil partner, in Inheritance Tax Act (IHTA) 1984, s 80, the term 'a qualifying interest in possession' is to be substituted for 'an interest in possession'.

This will mean that where one party to a couple succeeds to a life interest to which their spouse or civil partner was previously entitled during the latter's lifetime and that interest is not a transitional serial interest, IHTA 1984, s 80 will apply at that time (because neither spouse would then have a qualifying interest in possession) with the result that the settled property would be treated as being comprised in a settlement and therefore subject to the relevant property charges.

This change will apply from the date that Finance Bill 2015 receives Royal Assent.

Appointments for the benefit of the deceased's surviving partner

IHTA 1984, s 144 is to be amended so that the provisions of s 65(4), which prevent a charge to tax arising in the first three months after the settlement commenced, or within a 10-year anniversary, will not apply to appointments out of property settled by will. This will ensure that where an appointment is made within three months of the date of death in favour of the deceased's surviving spouse or civil partner, it can be read back into the will and exemption under s 18 can be given.

This change applies to all deaths on or after 10 December 2014.

Extending exemption for medals and other awards

The exclusion from IHT that applies to medals and other decorations that are awarded for valour and gallantry is being extended to all decorations and medals awarded by the Crown or by another country or territory outside the UK to the armed forces, emergency services personnel and to individuals in recognition of their achievements and service in public life.

The revised legislation will have effect in relation to transfers of value made or treated as made on or after 3 December 2014.

Exemption for emergency service personnel and humanitarian aid workers

Inheritance tax will not be charged on the estates of emergency service personnel and humanitarian aid workers whose death has been caused directly or hastened by injury or illness while responding to emergency circumstances. This change is effective for all deaths occurring on or after 19 March 2014.

Interest changes to support the new digital service

HMRC are currently developing a new service enabling people to submit inheritance tax (IHT) returns and settle any tax due online. The new service is expected to be available from 2015/16 onwards. In conjunction with this, amendments are being made to the existing IHT legislation relating to late payment interest, which will:

- extend the power to make regulations to allow the instalment interest provisions relating to certain financial institutions and companies to be updated; and
- clarify the period from when interest is charged.

Anti-avoidance, fairness and planning

Charities: status for tax purposes of certain bodies

From the date of Royal Assent to Finance Bill 2015, the Commonwealth War Graves Commission (CWGC) and the Imperial War Graves Endowment Fund Trustees will be treated as charities for tax purposes.

Improving the operation of the construction industry scheme

A series of changes is being made to improve the operation of the construction industry scheme (CIS), including:

- a reduction of the turnover test limit to £100,000 in multiple directorships;
- the initial and annual compliance tests will focus on fewer obligations;
- the nil return obligation will be amended;
- joint ventures where there is already one member with gross status will be allowed easier access to gross payment status;
- earlier repayment to liquidators in insolvency proceedings will be allowed; and
- mandation of filing of CIS returns and online verification.

The changes will have effect on and after 6 April 2015 for nil returns, joint ventures and repayments in cases of insolvency; 6 April 2016 for mandating online filing of CIS returns and changes to gross payment status tests; and 6 April 2017 for mandating of online verification.

Summary of Budget Proposals 18 March 2015

Making it easier: digital tax accounts

The Government is set to replace tax returns with digital tax accounts, enabling taxpayers to register for new services, update their information and review tax calculations. Details concerning policy and administrative changes will be published later this year.

In addition, the Government will consult on a new payment process to support the use of digital tax accounts which allow tax and National Insurance contributions to be collected outside of pay as you earn and self-assessment.

Regulations to implement the UK's automatic exchange of information agreements

To meet the UK's obligations under the EU Revised Directive on Administrative Co-operation, and under Competent Authority Agreements with non-EU jurisdictions for the Common Reporting Standard, Treasury regulations will create due diligence and reporting obligations for UK financial institutions with effect from 1 January 2016. These will replace the UK's current implementing regulations for the US Foreign Account Tax Compliance Act (FATCA), from a date still to be determined.

Financial institutions will be required to identify accounts maintained for account holders who are tax resident in jurisdictions with which the UK has entered into exchange of information agreements, and collect and report information to HMRC in a specified manner on specified persons.

Direct recovery of debts due to HMRC from debtors' bank and building society accounts

Legislation will be introduced in a Finance Bill later in 2015, during the next Parliament, to allow HMRC to secure payment of tax and tax credit debts directly from debtors' bank and building society accounts in credit, including ISAs. This proposal has caused widespread concerns, and its implementation has been delayed to allow further consideration of safeguards needed to protect taxpayers.

Strengthening penalties for offshore non-compliance

The existing penalty regime for non-compliance involving an offshore matter is extended and updated. With effect from 1 April 2015, the offshore penalty regime includes inheritance tax; covers cases where the proceeds of domestic non-compliance are situated or held outside of the UK; and has four (instead of three) levels of penalty, where the existing lowest level will apply to territories that adopt automatic exchange of information under the OECD's common reporting standard. Territories will be re-classified in a new statutory instrument.

With effect from the date of Royal Assent to the Finance Bill 2015, the offshore penalty regime will include a new type of penalty to be triggered following a movement of offshore assets to continue evading tax.

Country-by-country reporting

With effect from the date of Royal Assent to Finance Bill 2015, the Treasury will have power to require multinational enterprises (MNEs) to make an annual country-by-country report to HMRC showing, for each tax jurisdiction in which they do business: (a) the amount of revenue, profit before income tax and income tax paid and accrued; and (b) their total employment, capital, retained earnings and tangible assets. MNEs will also be required to identify each entity within the group doing business in a particular tax jurisdiction, and provide a broad indication of the business activities of each entity.

Disclosure of tax avoidance schemes (DOTAS) regime changes

From the date of Royal Assent to the Finance Bill 2015 or by secondary legislation thereafter, the DOTAS regime is to be changed by updating the rules determining what has to be disclosed, changing the information that must be provided to HMRC, enabling HMRC to publish information about promoters and disclosed schemes, and establishing a taskforce to enforce the strengthened regime.

In summary:

- The rules defining promoters are being changed to ensure disclosure is made by persons resident in the UK where a promoter not resident in the UK fails to disclose.
- The penalty applicable to scheme users who fail to correctly report their use of the scheme to HMRC is increased.
- The descriptions of what has to be disclosed will be updated in regulations.
- HMRC will be able to publish information about promoters and disclosed schemes.
- An employer who enters into a scheme in relation to the employment of its employees will have to provide employees with the scheme reference number (SRN) and periodically provide HMRC with information about the employees.
- The period during which HMRC may issue an SRN is increased from 30 to 90 days.

- HMRC will be able to include additional information in the form used by promoters to provide the SRN to clients and by clients to provide the SRN to others.
- People will be able to provide information voluntarily to HMRC to assist in determining whether there has been a breach of any DOTAS rules.
- The changes will be extended to schemes avoiding National Insurance contributions.

Promoters of Tax Avoidance Schemes

From the date of Royal Assent to the Finance Bill 2015, the promoters of tax avoidance schemes (POTAS) regime is to be amended to allow HMRC to issue conduct notices to a broader range of connected persons under the common control of a promoter, and the three-year time limit for issuing notices to promoters who have failed to disclose avoidance schemes to HMRC under DOTAS will apply from the date when the failure comes to the attention of HMRC, rather than the date of the underlying failure.

National Insurance Contributions – From 6 April 2015

CLASS 1: EMPLOYED PERSONS (NOT CONTRACTED OUT)

Rate for **Employees:**

(a) Employees under state pension age

Earnings up to £155 p.w.	Nil
Earnings between £155 and £815 p.w.	12.0%
Earnings over £815 p.w.	2.0%

(b) Employees over state pension age — Nil

(c) Married women and widows liable at reduced rate

Earnings up to £155 p.w.	Nil
Earnings between £155 p.w. and £815 p.w	5.85%
Earnings over £815 p.w.	2.0%

Rate for **Employers:**

Employees aged under 21:

Earnings up to £815 p.w.	Nil
Earnings over £815 p.w.	13.8%

Employees aged over 21:

Earnings up to £156 p.w.	Nil
Earnings over £156 p.w.	13.8%

CLASS 1: EMPLOYED PERSONS (CONTRACTED OUT)

Rate for **Employees:**

(a) Employees under state pension age

Earnings up to £155 p.w.	Nil
Earnings between £155 and £815 p.w.	10.6%
Earnings over £815 p.w.	2.0%

Rebate on earnings from £112 and £155 p.w.	1.4%

(b) Employees over state pension age — Nil

(c) Married women and widows liable at reduced rate

Earnings up to £155 p.w.	Nil
Earnings between £155 p.w. and £815 p.w	5.85%
Earnings over £815 p.w.	2.0%

Rate for **Employers** operating a salary-related scheme

(a) Employees under state pension age

Earnings up to £156 p.w.	Nil
Earnings between £156 and £815 p.w.	10.4%
Earnings over £815 p.w.	13.8%

Rebate on earnings from £112 and £156 p.w.	3.4%

(b) Employees over state pension age	Not allowed to contract out
(c) Married women and widows liable at reduced rate	As (a) above

EMPLOYMENT ALLOWANCE

(extended from April 2015 to certain individuals employing carers)	£2,000 per year, per employer

CLASS 2: SELF-EMPLOYED PERSONS

Exemption claimable if anticipated earnings less than £5,965	£2.80 p.w.

CLASS 3: VOLUNTARY CONTRIBUTIONS	£14.10 p.w.

CLASS 4: SELF-EMPLOYED PERSONS

Rate payable on profits between £8,060 and £42,385 per year	9.0%
Over £42,385 per year	2.0%

(a) Payable on taxable income between £31,786 and £150,000.
(b) Payable on chargeable transfers over £325,000.

2015/16: Income Tax (a) 40%
Inheritance Tax (b)

£ or p	Tax £ or p	£ or p	Tax £ or p	£	Tax £	£	Tax £	£	Tax £	£	Tax £	£	Tax £	£	Tax £	£	Tax £	£	Tax £
1	0·40	51	20·40	101	40·40	151	60·40	201	80·40	251	100·40	301	120·40	351	140·40	401	160·40	451	180·40
2	0·80	52	20·80	102	40·80	152	60·80	202	80·80	252	100·80	302	120·80	352	140·80	402	160·80	452	180·80
3	1·20	53	21·20	103	41·20	153	61·20	203	81·20	253	101·20	303	121·20	353	141·20	403	161·20	453	181·20
4	1·60	54	21·60	104	41·60	154	61·60	204	81·60	254	101·60	304	121·60	354	141·60	404	161·60	454	181·60
5	2·00	55	22·00	105	42·00	155	62·00	205	82·00	255	102·00	305	122·00	355	142·00	405	162·00	455	182·00
6	2·40	56	22·40	106	42·40	156	62·40	206	82·40	256	102·40	306	122·40	356	142·40	406	162·40	456	182·40
7	2·80	57	22·80	107	42·80	157	62·80	207	82·80	257	102·80	307	122·80	357	142·80	407	162·80	457	182·80
8	3·20	58	23·20	108	43·20	158	63·20	208	83·20	258	103·20	308	123·20	358	143·20	408	163·20	458	183·20
9	3·60	59	23·60	109	43·60	159	63·60	209	83·60	259	103·60	309	123·60	359	143·60	409	163·60	459	183·60
10	4·00	60	24·00	110	44·00	160	64·00	210	84·00	260	104·00	310	124·00	360	144·00	410	164·00	460	184·00
11	4·40	61	24·40	111	44·40	161	64·40	211	84·40	261	104·40	311	124·40	361	144·40	411	164·40	461	184·40
12	4·80	62	24·80	112	44·80	162	64·80	212	84·80	262	104·80	312	124·80	362	144·80	412	164·80	462	184·80
13	5·20	63	25·20	113	45·20	163	65·20	213	85·20	263	105·20	313	125·20	363	145·20	413	165·20	463	185·20
14	5·60	64	25·60	114	45·60	164	65·60	214	85·60	264	105·60	314	125·60	364	145·60	414	165·60	464	185·60
15	6·00	65	26·00	115	46·00	165	66·00	215	86·00	265	106·00	315	126·00	365	146·00	415	166·00	465	186·00
16	6·40	66	26·40	116	46·40	166	66·40	216	86·40	266	106·40	316	126·40	366	146·40	416	166·40	466	186·40
17	6·80	67	26·80	117	46·80	167	66·80	217	86·80	267	106·80	317	126·80	367	146·80	417	166·80	467	186·80
18	7·20	68	27·20	118	47·20	168	67·20	218	87·20	268	107·20	318	127·20	368	147·20	418	167·20	468	187·20
19	7·60	69	27·60	119	47·60	169	67·60	219	87·60	269	107·60	319	127·60	369	147·60	419	167·60	469	187·60
20	8·00	70	28·00	120	48·00	170	68·00	220	88·00	270	108·00	320	128·00	370	148·00	420	168·00	470	188·00
21	8·40	71	28·40	121	48·40	171	68·40	221	88·40	271	108·40	321	128·40	371	148·40	421	168·40	471	188·40
22	8·80	72	28·80	122	48·80	172	68·80	222	88·80	272	108·80	322	128·80	372	148·80	422	168·80	472	188·80
23	9·20	73	29·20	123	49·20	173	69·20	223	89·20	273	109·20	323	129·20	373	149·20	423	169·20	473	189·20
24	9·60	74	29·60	124	49·60	174	69·60	224	89·60	274	109·60	324	129·60	374	149·60	424	169·60	474	189·60
25	10·00	75	30·00	125	50·00	175	70·00	225	90·00	275	110·00	325	130·00	375	150·00	425	170·00	475	190·00
26	10·40	76	30·40	126	50·40	176	70·40	226	90·40	276	110·40	326	130·40	376	150·40	426	170·40	476	190·40
27	10·80	77	30·80	127	50·80	177	70·80	227	90·80	277	110·80	327	130·80	377	150·80	427	170·80	477	190·80
28	11·20	78	31·20	128	51·20	178	71·20	228	91·20	278	111·20	328	131·20	378	151·20	428	171·20	478	191·20
29	11·60	79	31·60	129	51·60	179	71·60	229	91·60	279	111·60	329	131·60	379	151·60	429	171·60	479	191·60
30	12·00	80	32·00	130	52·00	180	72·00	230	92·00	280	112·00	330	132·00	380	152·00	430	172·00	480	192·00
31	12·40	81	32·40	131	52·40	181	72·40	231	92·40	281	112·40	331	132·40	381	152·40	431	172·40	481	192·40
32	12·80	82	32·80	132	52·80	182	72·80	232	92·80	282	112·80	332	132·80	382	152·80	432	172·80	482	192·80
33	13·20	83	33·20	133	53·20	183	73·20	233	93·20	283	113·20	333	133·20	383	153·20	433	173·20	483	193·20
34	13·60	84	33·60	134	53·60	184	73·60	234	93·60	284	113·60	334	133·60	384	153·60	434	173·60	484	193·60
35	14·00	85	34·00	135	54·00	185	74·00	235	94·00	285	114·00	335	134·00	385	154·00	435	174·00	485	194·00
36	14·40	86	34·40	136	54·40	186	74·40	236	94·40	286	114·40	336	134·40	386	154·40	436	174·40	486	194·40
37	14·80	87	34·80	137	54·80	187	74·80	237	94·80	287	114·80	337	134·80	387	154·80	437	174·80	487	194·80
38	15·20	88	35·20	138	55·20	188	75·20	238	95·20	288	115·20	338	135·20	388	155·20	438	175·20	488	195·20
39	15·60	89	35·60	139	55·60	189	75·60	239	95·60	289	115·60	339	135·60	389	155·60	439	175·60	489	195·60
40	16·00	90	36·00	140	56·00	190	76·00	240	96·00	290	116·00	340	136·00	390	156·00	440	176·00	490	196·00
41	16·40	91	36·40	141	56·40	191	76·40	241	96·40	291	116·40	341	136·40	391	156·40	441	176·40	491	196·40
42	16·80	92	36·80	142	56·80	192	76·80	242	96·80	292	116·80	342	136·80	392	156·80	442	176·80	492	196·80
43	17·20	93	37·20	143	57·20	193	77·20	243	97·20	293	117·20	343	137·20	393	157·20	443	177·20	493	197·20
44	17·60	94	37·60	144	57·60	194	77·60	244	97·60	294	117·60	344	137·60	394	157·60	444	177·60	494	197·60
45	18·00	95	38·00	145	58·00	195	78·00	245	98·00	295	118·00	345	138·00	395	158·00	445	178·00	495	198·00
46	18·40	96	38·40	146	58·40	196	78·40	246	98·40	296	118·40	346	138·40	396	158·40	446	178·40	496	198·40
47	18·80	97	38·80	147	58·80	197	78·80	247	98·80	297	118·80	347	138·80	397	158·80	447	178·80	497	198·80
48	19·20	98	39·20	148	59·20	198	79·20	248	99·20	298	119·20	348	139·20	398	159·20	448	179·20	498	199·20
49	19·60	99	39·60	149	59·60	199	79·60	249	99·60	299	119·60	349	139·60	399	159·60	449	179·60	499	199·60
50	20·00	100	40·00	150	60·00	200	80·00	250	100·00	300	120·00	350	140·00	400	160·00	450	180·00	500	200·00

On Tax	£1,000 £400	£1,500 £600	£2,000 £800	£2,500 £1,000	£3,000 £1,200	£3,500 £1,400	£4,000 £1,600	£4,500 £1,800	£5,000 £2,000

45% 2015/16: Income Tax (a) Trusts (b)

(a) Additional rate payable on taxable income over £150,000.
(b) Trust rate

£ or p	Tax £ or p	£ or p	Tax £ or p	£	Tax £	£	Tax £	£	Tax £	£	Tax £	£	Tax £	£	Tax £	£	Tax £	£	Tax £
1	0.45	51	22.95	101	45.45	151	67.95	201	90.45	251	112.95	301	135.45	351	157.95	401	180.45	451	202.95
2	0.90	52	23.40	102	45.90	152	68.40	202	90.90	252	113.40	302	135.90	352	158.40	402	180.90	452	203.40
3	1.35	53	23.85	103	46.35	153	68.85	203	91.35	253	113.85	303	136.35	353	158.85	403	181.35	453	203.85
4	1.80	54	24.30	104	46.80	154	69.30	204	91.80	254	114.30	304	136.80	354	159.30	404	181.80	454	204.30
5	2.25	55	24.75	105	47.25	155	69.75	205	92.25	255	114.75	305	137.25	355	159.75	405	182.25	455	204.75
6	2.70	56	25.20	106	47.70	156	70.20	206	92.70	256	115.20	306	137.70	356	160.20	406	182.70	456	205.20
7	3.15	57	25.65	107	48.15	157	70.65	207	93.15	257	115.65	307	138.15	357	160.65	407	183.15	457	205.65
8	3.60	58	26.10	108	48.60	158	71.10	208	93.60	258	116.10	308	138.60	358	161.10	408	183.60	458	206.10
9	4.05	59	26.55	109	49.05	159	71.55	209	94.05	259	116.55	309	139.05	359	161.55	409	184.05	459	206.55
10	4.50	60	27.00	110	49.50	160	72.00	210	94.50	260	117.00	310	139.50	360	162.00	410	184.50	460	207.00
11	4.95	61	27.45	111	49.95	161	72.45	211	94.95	261	117.45	311	139.95	361	162.45	411	184.95	461	207.45
12	5.40	62	27.90	112	50.40	162	72.90	212	95.40	262	117.90	312	140.40	362	162.90	412	185.40	462	207.90
13	5.85	63	28.35	113	50.85	163	73.35	213	95.85	263	118.35	313	140.85	363	163.35	413	185.85	463	208.35
14	6.30	64	28.80	114	51.30	164	73.80	214	96.30	264	118.80	314	141.30	364	163.80	414	186.30	464	208.80
15	6.75	65	29.25	115	51.75	165	74.25	215	96.75	265	119.25	315	141.75	365	164.25	415	186.75	465	209.25
16	7.20	66	29.70	116	52.20	166	74.70	216	97.20	266	119.70	316	142.20	366	164.70	416	187.20	466	209.70
17	7.65	67	30.15	117	52.65	167	75.15	217	97.65	267	120.15	317	142.65	367	165.15	417	187.65	467	210.15
18	8.10	68	30.60	118	53.10	168	75.60	218	98.10	268	120.60	318	143.10	368	165.60	418	188.10	468	210.60
19	8.55	69	31.05	119	53.55	169	76.05	219	98.55	269	121.05	319	143.55	369	166.05	419	188.55	469	211.05
20	9.00	70	31.50	120	54.00	170	76.50	220	99.00	270	121.50	320	144.00	370	166.50	420	189.00	470	211.50
21	9.45	71	31.95	121	54.45	171	76.95	221	99.45	271	121.95	321	144.45	371	166.95	421	189.45	471	211.95
22	9.90	72	32.40	122	54.90	172	77.40	222	99.90	272	122.40	322	144.90	372	167.40	422	189.90	472	212.40
23	10.35	73	32.85	123	55.35	173	77.85	223	100.35	273	122.85	323	145.35	373	167.85	423	190.35	473	212.85
24	10.80	74	33.30	124	55.80	174	78.30	224	100.80	274	123.30	324	145.80	374	168.30	424	190.80	474	213.30
25	11.25	75	33.75	125	56.25	175	78.75	225	101.25	275	123.75	325	146.25	375	168.75	425	191.25	475	213.75
26	11.70	76	34.20	126	56.70	176	79.20	226	101.70	276	124.20	326	146.70	376	169.20	426	191.70	476	214.20
27	12.15	77	34.65	127	57.15	177	79.65	227	102.15	277	124.65	327	147.15	377	169.65	427	192.15	477	214.65
28	12.60	78	35.10	128	57.60	178	80.10	228	102.60	278	125.10	328	147.60	378	170.10	428	192.60	478	215.10
29	13.05	79	35.55	129	58.05	179	80.55	229	103.05	279	125.55	329	148.05	379	170.55	429	193.05	479	215.55
30	13.50	80	36.00	130	58.50	180	81.00	230	103.50	280	126.00	330	148.50	380	171.00	430	193.50	480	216.00
31	13.95	81	36.45	131	58.95	181	81.45	231	103.95	281	126.45	331	148.95	381	171.45	431	193.95	481	216.45
32	14.40	82	36.90	132	59.40	182	81.90	232	104.40	282	126.90	332	149.40	382	171.90	432	194.40	482	216.90
33	14.85	83	37.35	133	59.85	183	82.35	233	104.85	283	127.35	333	149.85	383	172.35	433	194.85	483	217.35
34	15.30	84	37.80	134	60.30	184	82.80	234	105.30	284	127.80	334	150.30	384	172.80	434	195.30	484	217.80
35	15.75	85	38.25	135	60.75	185	83.25	235	105.75	285	128.25	335	150.75	385	173.25	435	195.75	485	218.25
36	16.20	86	38.70	136	61.20	186	83.70	236	106.20	286	128.70	336	151.20	386	173.70	436	196.20	486	218.70
37	16.65	87	39.15	137	61.65	187	84.15	237	106.65	287	129.15	337	151.65	387	174.15	437	196.65	487	219.15
38	17.10	88	39.60	138	62.10	188	84.60	238	107.10	288	129.60	338	152.10	388	174.60	438	197.10	488	219.60
39	17.55	89	40.05	139	62.55	189	85.05	239	107.55	289	130.05	339	152.55	389	175.05	439	197.55	489	220.05
40	18.00	90	40.50	140	63.00	190	85.50	240	108.00	290	130.50	340	153.00	390	175.50	440	198.00	490	220.50
41	18.45	91	40.95	141	63.45	191	85.95	241	108.45	291	130.95	341	153.45	391	175.95	441	198.45	491	220.95
42	18.90	92	41.40	142	63.90	192	86.40	242	108.90	292	131.40	342	153.90	392	176.40	442	198.90	492	221.40
43	19.35	93	41.85	143	64.35	193	86.85	243	109.35	293	131.85	343	154.35	393	176.85	443	199.35	493	221.85
44	19.80	94	42.30	144	64.80	194	87.30	244	109.80	294	132.30	344	154.80	394	177.30	444	199.80	494	222.30
45	20.25	95	42.75	145	65.25	195	87.75	245	110.25	295	132.75	345	155.25	395	177.75	445	200.25	495	222.75
46	20.70	96	43.20	146	65.70	196	88.20	246	110.70	296	133.20	346	155.70	396	178.20	446	200.70	496	223.20
47	21.15	97	43.65	147	66.15	197	88.65	247	111.15	297	133.65	347	156.15	397	178.65	447	201.15	497	223.65
48	21.60	98	44.10	148	66.60	198	89.10	248	111.60	298	134.10	348	156.60	398	179.10	448	201.60	498	224.10
49	22.05	99	44.55	149	67.05	199	89.55	249	112.05	299	134.55	349	157.05	399	179.55	449	202.05	499	224.55
50	22.50	100	45.00	150	67.50	200	90.00	250	112.50	300	135.00	350	157.50	400	180.00	450	202.50	500	225.00
On Tax		**£1,000** £450		**£1,500** £675		**£2,000** £900		**£2,500** £1,125		**£3,000** £1,350		**£3,500** £1,575		**£4,000** £1,800		**£4,500** £2,025		**£5,000** £2,250	

Dividend Tax Credits 10%

£ or p	Tax £ or p	£ or p	Tax £ or p	£	Tax £	£	Tax £	£	Tax £	£	Tax £	£	Tax £	£	Tax £	£	Tax £	£	Tax £
1	0·11	51	5·67	101	11·22	151	16·78	201	22·33	251	27·89	301	33·44	351	39·00	401	44·56	451	50·11
2	0·22	52	5·78	102	11·33	152	16·89	202	22·44	252	28·00	302	33·56	352	39·11	402	44·67	452	50·22
3	0·33	53	5·89	103	11·44	153	17·00	203	22·56	253	28·11	303	33·67	353	39·22	403	44·78	453	50·33
4	0·44	54	6·00	104	11·56	154	17·11	204	22·67	254	28·22	304	33·78	354	39·33	404	44·89	454	50·44
5	0·56	55	6·11	105	11·67	155	17·22	205	22·78	255	28·33	305	33·89	355	39·44	405	45·00	455	50·56
6	0·67	56	6·22	106	11·78	156	17·33	206	22·89	256	28·44	306	34·00	356	39·56	406	45·11	456	50·67
7	0·78	57	6·33	107	11·89	157	17·44	207	23·00	257	28·56	307	34·11	357	39·67	407	45·22	457	50·78
8	0·89	58	6·44	108	12·00	158	17·56	208	23·11	258	28·67	308	34·22	358	39·78	408	45·33	458	50·89
9	1·00	59	6·56	109	12·11	159	17·67	209	23·22	259	28·78	309	34·33	359	39·89	409	45·44	459	51·00
10	1·11	60	6·67	110	12·22	160	17·78	210	23·33	260	28·89	310	34·44	360	40·00	410	45·56	460	51·11
11	1·22	61	6·78	111	12·33	161	17·89	211	23·44	261	29·00	311	34·56	361	40·11	411	45·67	461	51·22
12	1·33	62	6·89	112	12·44	162	18·00	212	23·56	262	29·11	312	34·67	362	40·22	412	45·78	462	51·33
13	1·44	63	7·00	113	12·56	163	18·11	213	23·67	263	29·22	313	34·78	363	40·33	413	45·89	463	51·44
14	1·56	64	7·11	114	12·67	164	18·22	214	23·78	264	29·33	314	34·89	364	40·44	414	46·00	464	51·56
15	1·67	65	7·22	115	12·78	165	18·33	215	23·89	265	29·44	315	35·00	365	40·56	415	46·11	465	51·67
16	1·78	66	7·33	116	12·89	166	18·44	216	24·00	266	29·56	316	35·11	366	40·67	416	46·22	466	51·78
17	1·89	67	7·44	117	13·00	167	18·56	217	24·11	267	29·67	317	35·22	367	40·78	417	46·33	467	51·89
18	2·00	68	7·56	118	13·11	168	18·67	218	24·22	268	29·78	318	35·33	368	40·89	418	46·44	468	52·00
19	2·11	69	7·67	119	13·22	169	18·78	219	24·33	269	29·89	319	35·44	369	41·00	419	46·56	469	52·11
20	2·22	70	7·78	120	13·33	170	18·89	220	24·44	270	30·00	320	35·56	370	41·11	420	46·67	470	52·22
21	2·33	71	7·89	121	13·44	171	19·00	221	24·56	271	30·11	321	35·67	371	41·22	421	46·78	471	52·33
22	2·44	72	8·00	122	13·56	172	19·11	222	24·67	272	30·22	322	35·78	372	41·33	422	46·89	472	52·44
23	2·56	73	8·11	123	13·67	173	19·22	223	24·78	273	30·33	323	35·89	373	41·44	423	47·00	473	52·56
24	2·67	74	8·22	124	13·78	174	19·33	224	24·89	274	30·44	324	36·00	374	41·56	424	47·11	474	52·67
25	2·78	75	8·33	125	13·89	175	19·44	225	25·00	275	30·56	325	36·11	375	41·67	425	47·22	475	52·78
26	2·89	76	8·44	126	14·00	176	19·56	226	25·11	276	30·67	326	36·22	376	41·78	426	47·33	476	52·89
27	3·00	77	8·56	127	14·11	177	19·67	227	25·22	277	30·78	327	36·33	377	41·89	427	47·44	477	53·00
28	3·11	78	8·67	128	14·22	178	19·78	228	25·33	278	30·89	328	36·44	378	42·00	428	47·56	478	53·11
29	3·22	79	8·78	129	14·33	179	19·89	229	25·44	279	31·00	329	36·56	379	42·11	429	47·67	479	53·22
30	3·33	80	8·89	130	14·44	180	20·00	230	25·56	280	31·11	330	36·67	380	42·22	430	47·78	480	53·33
31	3·44	81	9·00	131	14·56	181	20·11	231	25·67	281	31·22	331	36·78	381	42·33	431	47·89	481	53·44
32	3·56	82	9·11	132	14·67	182	20·22	232	25·78	282	31·33	332	36·89	382	42·44	432	48·00	482	53·56
33	3·67	83	9·22	133	14·78	183	20·33	233	25·89	283	31·44	333	37·00	383	42·56	433	48·11	483	53·67
34	3·78	84	9·33	134	14·89	184	20·44	234	26·00	284	31·56	334	37·11	384	42·67	434	48·22	484	53·78
35	3·89	85	9·44	135	15·00	185	20·56	235	26·11	285	31·67	335	37·22	385	42·78	435	48·33	485	53·89
36	4·00	86	9·56	136	15·11	186	20·67	236	26·22	286	31·78	336	37·33	386	42·89	436	48·44	486	54·00
37	4·11	87	9·67	137	15·22	187	20·78	237	26·33	287	31·89	337	37·44	387	43·00	437	48·56	487	54·11
38	4·22	88	9·78	138	15·33	188	20·89	238	26·44	288	32·00	338	37·56	388	43·11	438	48·67	488	54·22
39	4·33	89	9·89	139	15·44	189	21·00	239	26·56	289	32·11	339	37·67	389	43·22	439	48·78	489	54·33
40	4·44	90	10·00	140	15·56	190	21·11	240	26·67	290	32·22	340	37·78	390	43·33	440	48·89	490	54·44
41	4·56	91	10·11	141	15·67	191	21·22	241	26·78	291	32·33	341	37·89	391	43·44	441	49·00	491	54·56
42	4·67	92	10·22	142	15·78	192	21·33	242	26·89	292	32·44	342	38·00	392	43·56	442	49·11	492	54·67
43	4·78	93	10·33	143	15·89	193	21·44	243	27·00	293	32·56	343	38·11	393	43·67	443	49·22	493	54·78
44	4·89	94	10·44	144	16·00	194	21·56	244	27·11	294	32·67	344	38·22	394	43·78	444	49·33	494	54·89
45	5·00	95	10·56	145	16·11	195	21·67	245	27·22	295	32·78	345	38·33	395	43·89	445	49·44	495	55·00
46	5·11	96	10·67	146	16·22	196	21·78	246	27·33	296	32·89	346	38·44	396	44·00	446	49·56	496	55·11
47	5·22	97	10·78	147	16·33	197	21·89	247	27·44	297	33·00	347	38·56	397	44·11	447	49·67	497	55·22
48	5·33	98	10·89	148	16·44	198	22·00	248	27·56	298	33·11	348	38·67	398	44·22	448	49·78	498	55·33
49	5·44	99	11·00	149	16·56	199	22·11	249	27·67	299	33·22	349	38·78	399	44·33	449	49·89	499	55·44
50	5·56	100	11·11	150	16·67	200	22·22	250	27·78	300	33·33	350	38·89	400	44·44	450	50·00	500	55·56

On Tax	£1,000 £111	£1,500 £167	£2,000 £222	£2,500 £278	£3,000 £333	£3,500 £389	£4,000 £444	£4,500 £500	£5,000 £556

32·5%   Dividend Tax Credits

£ or p	Tax £ or p	£ or p	Tax £ or p	£	Tax £	£	Tax £	£	Tax £	£	Tax £	£	Tax £	£	Tax £	£	Tax £	£	Tax £
1	0·48	51	24·56	101	48·63	151	72·70	201	96·78	251	120·85	301	144·93	351	169·00	401	193·07	451	217·15
2	0·96	52	25·04	102	49·11	152	73·19	202	97·26	252	121·33	302	145·41	352	169·48	402	193·56	452	217·63
3	1·44	53	25·52	103	49·59	153	73·67	203	97·74	253	121·81	303	145·89	353	169·96	403	194·04	453	218·11
4	1·93	54	26·00	104	50·07	154	74·15	204	98·22	254	122·30	304	146·37	354	170·44	404	194·52	454	218·59
5	2·41	55	26·48	105	50·56	155	74·63	205	98·70	255	122·78	305	146·85	355	170·93	405	195·00	455	219·07
6	2·89	56	26·96	106	51·04	156	75·11	206	99·19	256	123·26	306	147·33	356	171·41	406	195·48	456	219·56
7	3·37	57	27·44	107	51·52	157	75·59	207	99·67	257	123·74	307	147·81	357	171·89	407	195·96	457	220·04
8	3·85	58	27·93	108	52·00	158	76·07	208	100·15	258	124·22	308	148·30	358	172·37	408	196·44	458	220·52
9	4·33	59	28·41	109	52·48	159	76·56	209	100·63	259	124·70	309	148·78	359	172·85	409	196·93	459	221·00
10	4·81	60	28·89	110	52·96	160	77·04	210	101·11	260	125·19	310	149·26	360	173·33	410	197·41	460	221·48
11	5·30	61	29·37	111	53·44	161	77·52	211	101·59	261	125·67	311	149·74	361	173·81	411	197·89	461	221·96
12	5·78	62	29·85	112	53·93	162	78·00	212	102·07	262	126·15	312	150·22	362	174·30	412	198·37	462	222·44
13	6·26	63	30·33	113	54·41	163	78·48	213	102·56	263	126·63	313	150·70	363	174·78	413	198·85	463	222·93
14	6·74	64	30·81	114	54·89	164	78·96	214	103·04	264	127·11	314	151·19	364	175·26	414	199·33	464	223·41
15	7·22	65	31·30	115	55·37	165	79·44	215	103·52	265	127·59	315	151·67	365	175·74	415	199·81	465	223·89
16	7·70	66	31·78	116	55·85	166	79·93	216	104·00	266	128·07	316	152·15	366	176·22	416	200·30	466	224·37
17	8·19	67	32·26	117	56·33	167	80·41	217	104·48	267	128·56	317	152·63	367	176·70	417	200·78	467	224·85
18	8·67	68	32·74	118	56·81	168	80·89	218	104·96	268	129·04	318	153·11	368	177·19	418	201·26	468	225·33
19	9·15	69	33·22	119	57·30	169	81·37	219	105·44	269	129·52	319	153·59	369	177·67	419	201·74	469	225·81
20	9·63	70	33·70	120	57·78	170	81·85	220	105·93	270	130·00	320	154·07	370	178·15	420	202·22	470	226·30
21	10·11	71	34·19	121	58·26	171	82·33	221	106·41	271	130·48	321	154·56	371	178·63	421	202·70	471	226·78
22	10·59	72	34·67	122	58·74	172	82·81	222	106·89	272	130·96	322	155·04	372	179·11	422	203·19	472	227·26
23	11·07	73	35·15	123	59·22	173	83·30	223	107·37	273	131·44	323	155·52	373	179·59	423	203·67	473	227·74
24	11·56	74	35·63	124	59·70	174	83·78	224	107·85	274	131·93	324	156·00	374	180·07	424	204·15	474	228·22
25	12·04	75	36·11	125	60·19	175	84·26	225	108·33	275	132·41	325	156·48	375	180·56	425	204·63	475	228·70
26	12·52	76	36·59	126	60·67	176	84·74	226	108·81	276	132·89	326	156·96	376	181·04	426	205·11	476	229·19
27	13·00	77	37·07	127	61·15	177	85·22	227	109·30	277	133·37	327	157·44	377	181·52	427	205·59	477	229·67
28	13·48	78	37·56	128	61·63	178	85·70	228	109·78	278	133·85	328	157·93	378	182·00	428	206·07	478	230·15
29	13·96	79	38·04	129	62·11	179	86·19	229	110·26	279	134·33	329	158·41	379	182·48	429	206·56	479	230·63
30	14·44	80	38·52	130	62·59	180	86·67	230	110·74	280	134·81	330	158·89	380	182·96	430	207·04	480	231·11
31	14·93	81	39·00	131	63·07	181	87·15	231	111·22	281	135·30	331	159·37	381	183·44	431	207·52	481	231·59
32	15·41	82	39·48	132	63·56	182	87·63	232	111·70	282	135·78	332	159·85	382	183·93	432	208·00	482	232·07
33	15·89	83	39·96	133	64·04	183	88·11	233	112·19	283	136·26	333	160·33	383	184·41	433	208·48	483	232·56
34	16·37	84	40·44	134	64·52	184	88·59	234	112·67	284	136·74	334	160·81	384	184·89	434	208·96	484	233·04
35	16·85	85	40·93	135	65·00	185	89·07	235	113·15	285	137·22	335	161·30	385	185·37	435	209·44	485	233·52
36	17·33	86	41·41	136	65·48	186	89·56	236	113·63	286	137·70	336	161·78	386	185·85	436	209·93	486	234·00
37	17·81	87	41·89	137	65·96	187	90·04	237	114·11	287	138·19	337	162·26	387	186·33	437	210·41	487	234·48
38	18·30	88	42·37	138	66·44	188	90·52	238	114·59	288	138·67	338	162·74	388	186·81	438	210·89	488	234·96
39	18·78	89	42·85	139	66·93	189	91·00	239	115·07	289	139·15	339	163·22	389	187·30	439	211·37	489	235·44
40	19·26	90	43·33	140	67·41	190	91·48	240	115·56	290	139·63	340	163·70	390	187·78	440	211·85	490	235·93
41	19·74	91	43·81	141	67·89	191	91·96	241	116·04	291	140·11	341	164·19	391	188·26	441	212·33	491	236·41
42	20·22	92	44·30	142	68·37	192	92·44	242	116·52	292	140·59	342	164·67	392	188·74	442	212·81	492	236·89
43	20·70	93	44·78	143	68·85	193	92·93	243	117·00	293	141·07	343	165·15	393	189·22	443	213·30	493	237·37
44	21·19	94	45·26	144	69·33	194	93·41	244	117·48	294	141·56	344	165·63	394	189·70	444	213·78	494	237·85
45	21·67	95	45·74	145	69·81	195	93·89	245	117·96	295	142·04	345	166·11	395	190·19	445	214·26	495	238·33
46	22·15	96	46·22	146	70·30	196	94·37	246	118·44	296	142·52	346	166·59	396	190·67	446	214·74	496	238·81
47	22·63	97	46·70	147	70·78	197	94·85	247	118·93	297	143·00	347	167·07	397	191·15	447	215·22	497	239·30
48	23·11	98	47·19	148	71·26	198	95·33	248	119·41	298	143·48	348	167·56	398	191·63	448	215·70	498	239·78
49	23·59	99	47·67	149	71·74	199	95·81	249	119·89	299	143·96	349	168·04	399	192·11	449	216·19	499	240·26
50	24·07	100	48·15	150	72·22	200	96·30	250	120·37	300	144·44	350	168·52	400	192·59	450	216·67	500	240·74
On Tax		**£1,000** £481		**£1,500** £722		**£2,000** £963		**£2,500** £1,204		**£3,000** £1,444		**£3,500** £1,685		**£4,000** £1,926		**£4,500** £2,167		**£5,000** £2,407	

Dividend Tax Credits   37·5%

£ or p	Tax £ or p	£ or p	Tax £ or p	£	Tax £	£	Tax £	£	Tax £	£	Tax £	£	Tax £	£	Tax £	£	Tax £	£	Tax £
1	0·60	51	30·60	101	60·60	151	90·60	201	120·60	251	150·60	301	180·60	351	210·60	401	240·60	451	270·60
2	1·20	52	31·20	102	61·20	152	91·20	202	121·20	252	151·20	302	181·20	352	211·20	402	241·20	452	271·20
3	1·80	53	31·80	103	61·80	153	91·80	203	121·80	253	151·80	303	181·80	353	211·80	403	241·80	453	271·80
4	2·40	54	32·40	104	62·40	154	92·40	204	122·40	254	152·40	304	182·40	354	212·40	404	242·40	454	272·40
5	3·00	55	33·00	105	63·00	155	93·00	205	123·00	255	153·00	305	183·00	355	213·00	405	243·00	455	273·00
6	3·60	56	33·60	106	63·60	156	93·60	206	123·60	256	153·60	306	183·60	356	213·60	406	243·60	456	273·60
7	4·20	57	34·20	107	64·20	157	94·20	207	124·20	257	154·20	307	184·20	357	214·20	407	244·20	457	274·20
8	4·80	58	34·80	108	64·80	158	94·80	208	124·80	258	154·80	308	184·80	358	214·80	408	244·80	458	274·80
9	5·40	59	35·40	109	65·40	159	95·40	209	125·40	259	155·40	309	185·40	359	215·40	409	245·40	459	275·40
10	6·00	60	36·00	110	66·00	160	96·00	210	126·00	260	156·00	310	186·00	360	216·00	410	246·00	460	276·00
11	6·60	61	36·60	111	66·60	161	96·60	211	126·60	261	156·60	311	186·60	361	216·60	411	246·60	461	276·60
12	7·20	62	37·20	112	67·20	162	97·20	212	127·20	262	157·20	312	187·20	362	217·20	412	247·20	462	277·20
13	7·80	63	37·80	113	67·80	163	97·80	213	127·80	263	157·80	313	187·80	363	217·80	413	247·80	463	277·80
14	8·40	64	38·40	114	68·40	164	98·40	214	128·40	264	158·40	314	188·40	364	218·40	414	248·40	464	278·40
15	9·00	65	39·00	115	69·00	165	99·00	215	129·00	265	159·00	315	189·00	365	219·00	415	249·00	465	279·00
16	9·60	66	39·60	116	69·60	166	99·60	216	129·60	266	159·60	316	189·60	366	219·60	416	249·60	466	279·60
17	10·20	67	40·20	117	70·20	167	100·20	217	130·20	267	160·20	317	190·20	367	220·20	417	250·20	467	280·20
18	10·80	68	40·80	118	70·80	168	100·80	218	130·80	268	160·80	318	190·80	368	220·80	418	250·80	468	280·80
19	11·40	69	41·40	119	71·40	169	101·40	219	131·40	269	161·40	319	191·40	369	221·40	419	251·40	469	281·40
20	12·00	70	42·00	120	72·00	170	102·00	220	132·00	270	162·00	320	192·00	370	222·00	420	252·00	470	282·00
21	12·60	71	42·60	121	72·60	171	102·60	221	132·60	271	162·60	321	192·60	371	222·60	421	252·60	471	282·60
22	13·20	72	43·20	122	73·20	172	103·20	222	133·20	272	163·20	322	193·20	372	223·20	422	253·20	472	283·20
23	13·80	73	43·80	123	73·80	173	103·80	223	133·80	273	163·80	323	193·80	373	223·80	423	253·80	473	283·80
24	14·40	74	44·40	124	74·40	174	104·40	224	134·40	274	164·40	324	194·40	374	224·40	424	254·40	474	284·40
25	15·00	75	45·00	125	75·00	175	105·00	225	135·00	275	165·00	325	195·00	375	225·00	425	255·00	475	285·00
26	15·60	76	45·60	126	75·60	176	105·60	226	135·60	276	165·60	326	195·60	376	225·60	426	255·60	476	285·60
27	16·20	77	46·20	127	76·20	177	106·20	227	136·20	277	166·20	327	196·20	377	226·20	427	256·20	477	286·20
28	16·80	78	46·80	128	76·80	178	106·80	228	136·80	278	166·80	328	196·80	378	226·80	428	256·80	478	286·80
29	17·40	79	47·40	129	77·40	179	107·40	229	137·40	279	167·40	329	197·40	379	227·40	429	257·40	479	287·40
30	18·00	80	48·00	130	78·00	180	108·00	230	138·00	280	168·00	330	198·00	380	228·00	430	258·00	480	288·00
31	18·60	81	48·60	131	78·60	181	108·60	231	138·60	281	168·60	331	198·60	381	228·60	431	258·60	481	288·60
32	19·20	82	49·20	132	79·20	182	109·20	232	139·20	282	169·20	332	199·20	382	229·20	432	259·20	482	289·20
33	19·80	83	49·80	133	79·80	183	109·80	233	139·80	283	169·80	333	199·80	383	229·80	433	259·80	483	289·80
34	20·40	84	50·40	134	80·40	184	110·40	234	140·40	284	170·40	334	200·40	384	230·40	434	260·40	484	290·40
35	21·00	85	51·00	135	81·00	185	111·00	235	141·00	285	171·00	335	201·00	385	231·00	435	261·00	485	291·00
36	21·60	86	51·60	136	81·60	186	111·60	236	141·60	286	171·60	336	201·60	386	231·60	436	261·60	486	291·60
37	22·20	87	52·20	137	82·20	187	112·20	237	142·20	287	172·20	337	202·20	387	232·20	437	262·20	487	292·20
38	22·80	88	52·80	138	82·80	188	112·80	238	142·80	288	172·80	338	202·80	388	232·80	438	262·80	488	292·80
39	23·40	89	53·40	139	83·40	189	113·40	239	143·40	289	173·40	339	203·40	389	233·40	439	263·40	489	293·40
40	24·00	90	54·00	140	84·00	190	114·00	240	144·00	290	174·00	340	204·00	390	234·00	440	264·00	490	294·00
41	24·60	91	54·60	141	84·60	191	114·60	241	144·60	291	174·60	341	204·60	391	234·60	441	264·60	491	294·60
42	25·20	92	55·20	142	85·20	192	115·20	242	145·20	292	175·20	342	205·20	392	235·20	442	265·20	492	295·20
43	25·80	93	55·80	143	85·80	193	115·80	243	145·80	293	175·80	343	205·80	393	235·80	443	265·80	493	295·80
44	26·40	94	56·40	144	86·40	194	116·40	244	146·40	294	176·40	344	206·40	394	236·40	444	266·40	494	296·40
45	27·00	95	57·00	145	87·00	195	117·00	245	147·00	295	177·00	345	207·00	395	237·00	445	267·00	495	297·00
46	27·60	96	57·60	146	87·60	196	117·60	246	147·60	296	177·60	346	207·60	396	237·60	446	267·60	496	297·60
47	28·20	97	58·20	147	88·20	197	118·20	247	148·20	297	178·20	347	208·20	397	238·20	447	268·20	497	298·20
48	28·80	98	58·80	148	88·80	198	118·80	248	148·80	298	178·80	348	208·80	398	238·80	448	268·80	498	298·80
49	29·40	99	59·40	149	89·40	199	119·40	249	149·40	299	179·40	349	209·40	399	239·40	449	269·40	499	299·40
50	30·00	100	60·00	150	90·00	200	120·00	250	150·00	300	180·00	350	210·00	400	240·00	450	270·00	500	300·00
£1,000 £600		**£1,500** £900		**£2,000** £1,200		**£2,500** £1,500		**£3,000** £1,800		**£3,500** £2,100		**£4,000** £2,400		**£4,500** £2,700		**£5,000** £3,000		**£5,000** £3,000	

20%   VAT at Standard Rate

£ or p	Tax £ or p	£ or p	Tax £ or p	£	Tax £	£	Tax £	£	Tax £	£	Tax £	£	Tax £	£	Tax £	£	Tax £	£	Tax £
1	0·20	51	10·20	101	20·20	151	30·20	201	40·20	251	50·20	301	60·20	351	70·20	401	80·20	451	90·20
2	0·40	52	10·40	102	20·40	152	30·40	202	40·40	252	50·40	302	60·40	352	70·40	402	80·40	452	90·40
3	0·60	53	10·60	103	20·60	153	30·60	203	40·60	253	50·60	303	60·60	353	70·60	403	80·60	453	90·60
4	0·80	54	10·80	104	20·80	154	30·80	204	40·80	254	50·80	304	60·80	354	70·80	404	80·80	454	90·80
5	1·00	55	11·00	105	21·00	155	31·00	205	41·00	255	51·00	305	61·00	355	71·00	405	81·00	455	91·00
6	1·20	56	11·20	106	21·20	156	31·20	206	41·20	256	51·20	306	61·20	356	71·20	406	81·20	456	91·20
7	1·40	57	11·40	107	21·40	157	31·40	207	41·40	257	51·40	307	61·40	357	71·40	407	81·40	457	91·40
8	1·60	58	11·60	108	21·60	158	31·60	208	41·60	258	51·60	308	61·60	358	71·60	408	81·60	458	91·60
9	1·80	59	11·80	109	21·80	159	31·80	209	41·80	259	51·80	309	61·80	359	71·80	409	81·80	459	91·80
10	2·00	60	12·00	110	22·00	160	32·00	210	42·00	260	52·00	310	62·00	360	72·00	410	82·00	460	92·00
11	2·20	61	12·20	111	22·20	161	32·20	211	42·20	261	52·20	311	62·20	361	72·20	411	82·20	461	92·20
12	2·40	62	12·40	112	22·40	162	32·40	212	42·40	262	52·40	312	62·40	362	72·40	412	82·40	462	92·40
13	2·60	63	12·60	113	22·60	163	32·60	213	42·60	263	52·60	313	62·60	363	72·60	413	82·60	463	92·60
14	2·80	64	12·80	114	22·80	164	32·80	214	42·80	264	52·80	314	62·80	364	72·80	414	82·80	464	92·80
15	3·00	65	13·00	115	23·00	165	33·00	215	43·00	265	53·00	315	63·00	365	73·00	415	83·00	465	93·00
16	3·20	66	13·20	116	23·20	166	33·20	216	43·20	266	53·20	316	63·20	366	73·20	416	83·20	466	93·20
17	3·40	67	13·40	117	23·40	167	33·40	217	43·40	267	53·40	317	63·40	367	73·40	417	83·40	467	93·40
18	3·60	68	13·60	118	23·60	168	33·60	218	43·60	268	53·60	318	63·60	368	73·60	418	83·60	468	93·60
19	3·80	69	13·80	119	23·80	169	33·80	219	43·80	269	53·80	319	63·80	369	73·80	419	83·80	469	93·80
20	4·00	70	14·00	120	24·00	170	34·00	220	44·00	270	54·00	320	64·00	370	74·00	420	84·00	470	94·00
21	4·20	71	14·20	121	24·20	171	34·20	221	44·20	271	54·20	321	64·20	371	74·20	421	84·20	471	94·20
22	4·40	72	14·40	122	24·40	172	34·40	222	44·40	272	54·40	322	64·40	372	74·40	422	84·40	472	94·40
23	4·60	73	14·60	123	24·60	173	34·60	223	44·60	273	54·60	323	64·60	373	74·60	423	84·60	473	94·60
24	4·80	74	14·80	124	24·80	174	34·80	224	44·80	274	54·80	324	64·80	374	74·80	424	84·80	474	94·80
25	5·00	75	15·00	125	25·00	175	35·00	225	45·00	275	55·00	325	65·00	375	75·00	425	85·00	475	95·00
26	5·20	76	15·20	126	25·20	176	35·20	226	45·20	276	55·20	326	65·20	376	75·20	426	85·20	476	95·20
27	5·40	77	15·40	127	25·40	177	35·40	227	45·40	277	55·40	327	65·40	377	75·40	427	85·40	477	95·40
28	5·60	78	15·60	128	25·60	178	35·60	228	45·60	278	55·60	328	65·60	378	75·60	428	85·60	478	95·60
29	5·80	79	15·80	129	25·80	179	35·80	229	45·80	279	55·80	329	65·80	379	75·80	429	85·80	479	95·80
30	6·00	80	16·00	130	26·00	180	36·00	230	46·00	280	56·00	330	66·00	380	76·00	430	86·00	480	96·00
31	6·20	81	16·20	131	26·20	181	36·20	231	46·20	281	56·20	331	66·20	381	76·20	431	86·20	481	96·20
32	6·40	82	16·40	132	26·40	182	36·40	232	46·40	282	56·40	332	66·40	382	76·40	432	86·40	482	96·40
33	6·60	83	16·60	133	26·60	183	36·60	233	46·60	283	56·60	333	66·60	383	76·60	433	86·60	483	96·60
34	6·80	84	16·80	134	26·80	184	36·80	234	46·80	284	56·80	334	66·80	384	76·80	434	86·80	484	96·80
35	7·00	85	17·00	135	27·00	185	37·00	235	47·00	285	57·00	335	67·00	385	77·00	435	87·00	485	97·00
36	7·20	86	17·20	136	27·20	186	37·20	236	47·20	286	57·20	336	67·20	386	77·20	436	87·20	486	97·20
37	7·40	87	17·40	137	27·40	187	37·40	237	47·40	287	57·40	337	67·40	387	77·40	437	87·40	487	97·40
38	7·60	88	17·60	138	27·60	188	37·60	238	47·60	288	57·60	338	67·60	388	77·60	438	87·60	488	97·60
39	7·80	89	17·80	139	27·80	189	37·80	239	47·80	289	57·80	339	67·80	389	77·80	439	87·80	489	97·80
40	8·00	90	18·00	140	28·00	190	38·00	240	48·00	290	58·00	340	68·00	390	78·00	440	88·00	490	98·00
41	8·20	91	18·20	141	28·20	191	38·20	241	48·20	291	58·20	341	68·20	391	78·20	441	88·20	491	98·20
42	8·40	92	18·40	142	28·40	192	38·40	242	48·40	292	58·40	342	68·40	392	78·40	442	88·40	492	98·40
43	8·60	93	18·60	143	28·60	193	38·60	243	48·60	293	58·60	343	68·60	393	78·60	443	88·60	493	98·60
44	8·80	94	18·80	144	28·80	194	38·80	244	48·80	294	58·80	344	68·80	394	78·80	444	88·80	494	98·80
45	9·00	95	19·00	145	29·00	195	39·00	245	49·00	295	59·00	345	69·00	395	79·00	445	89·00	495	99·00
46	9·20	96	19·20	146	29·20	196	39·20	246	49·20	296	59·20	346	69·20	396	79·20	446	89·20	496	99·20
47	9·40	97	19·40	147	29·40	197	39·40	247	49·40	297	59·40	347	69·40	397	79·40	447	89·40	497	99·40
48	9·60	98	19·60	148	29·60	198	39·60	248	49·60	298	59·60	348	69·60	398	79·60	448	89·60	498	99·60
49	9·80	99	19·80	149	29·80	199	39·80	249	49·80	299	59·80	349	69·80	399	79·80	449	89·80	499	99·80
50	10·00	100	20·00	150	30·00	200	40·00	250	50·00	300	60·00	350	70·00	400	80·00	450	90·00	500	100·00

On	£1,000	£1,500	£2,000	£2,500	£3,000	£3,500	£4,000	£4,500	£5,000
Tax	£200	£300	£400	£500	£600	£700	£800	£900	£1,000

VAT Content of Inclusive Prices   20%

Inclusive Price £ or p	VAT @20% £ or p	Basic Price £ or p	Inclusive Price £ or p	VAT @20% £ or p	Basic Price £ or p	Inclusive Price £ or p	VAT @20% £ or p	Basic Price £ or p	Inclusive Price £ or p	VAT @20% £ or p	Basic Price £ or p	Inclusive Price £ or p	VAT @20% £ or p	Basic Price £ or p	Inclusive Price £ or p	VAT @20% £ or p	Basic Price £ or p
1	0·17	0·83	51	8·50	42·50	101	16·83	84·17	151	25·17	125·83	201	33·50	167·50	251	41·83	209·17
2	0·33	1·67	52	8·67	43·33	102	17·00	85·00	152	25·33	126·67	202	33·67	168·33	252	42·00	210·00
3	0·50	2·50	53	8·83	44·17	103	17·17	85·83	153	25·50	127·50	203	33·83	169·17	253	42·17	210·83
4	0·67	3·33	54	9·00	45·00	104	17·33	86·67	154	25·67	128·33	204	34·00	170·00	254	42·33	211·67
5	0·83	4·17	55	9·17	45·83	105	17·50	87·50	155	25·83	129·17	205	34·17	170·83	255	42·50	212·50
6	1·00	5·00	56	9·33	46·67	106	17·67	88·33	156	26·00	130·00	206	34·33	171·67	256	42·67	213·33
7	1·17	5·83	57	9·50	47·50	107	17·83	89·17	157	26·17	130·83	207	34·50	172·50	257	42·83	214·17
8	1·33	6·67	58	9·67	48·33	108	18·00	90·00	158	26·33	131·67	208	34·67	173·33	258	43·00	215·00
9	1·50	7·50	59	9·83	49·17	109	18·17	90·83	159	26·50	132·50	209	34·83	174·17	259	43·17	215·83
10	1·67	8·33	60	10·00	50·00	110	18·33	91·67	160	26·67	133·33	210	35·00	175·00	260	43·33	216·67
11	1·83	9·17	61	10·17	50·83	111	18·50	92·50	161	26·83	134·17	211	35·17	175·83	261	43·50	217·50
12	2·00	10·00	62	10·33	51·67	112	18·67	93·33	162	27·00	135·00	212	35·33	176·67	262	43·67	218·33
13	2·17	10·83	63	10·50	52·50	113	18·83	94·17	163	27·17	135·83	213	35·50	177·50	263	43·83	219·17
14	2·33	11·67	64	10·67	53·33	114	19·00	95·00	164	27·33	136·67	214	35·67	178·33	264	44·00	220·00
15	2·50	12·50	65	10·83	54·17	115	19·17	95·83	165	27·50	137·50	215	35·83	179·17	265	44·17	220·83
16	2·67	13·33	66	11·00	55·00	116	19·33	96·67	166	27·67	138·33	216	36·00	180·00	266	44·33	221·67
17	2·83	14·17	67	11·17	55·83	117	19·50	97·50	167	27·83	139·17	217	36·17	180·83	267	44·50	222·50
18	3·00	15·00	68	11·33	56·67	118	19·67	98·33	168	28·00	140·00	218	36·33	181·67	268	44·67	223·33
19	3·17	15·83	69	11·50	57·50	119	19·83	99·17	169	28·17	140·83	219	36·50	182·50	269	44·83	224·17
20	3·33	16·67	70	11·67	58·33	120	20·00	100·00	170	28·33	141·67	220	36·67	183·33	270	45·00	225·00
21	3·50	17·50	71	11·83	59·17	121	20·17	100·83	171	28·50	142·50	221	36·83	184·17	271	45·17	225·83
22	3·67	18·33	72	12·00	60·00	122	20·33	101·67	172	28·67	143·33	222	37·00	185·00	272	45·33	226·67
23	3·83	19·17	73	12·17	60·83	123	20·50	102·50	173	28·83	144·17	223	37·17	185·83	273	45·50	227·50
24	4·00	20·00	74	12·33	61·67	124	20·67	103·33	174	29·00	145·00	224	37·33	186·67	274	45·67	228·33
25	4·17	20·83	75	12·50	62·50	125	20·83	104·17	175	29·17	145·83	225	37·50	187·50	275	45·83	229·17
26	4·33	21·67	76	12·67	63·33	126	21·00	105·00	176	29·33	146·67	226	37·67	188·33	276	46·00	230·00
27	4·50	22·50	77	12·83	64·17	127	21·17	105·83	177	29·50	147·50	227	37·83	189·17	277	46·17	230·83
28	4·67	23·33	78	13·00	65·00	128	21·33	106·67	178	29·67	148·33	228	38·00	190·00	278	46·33	231·67
29	4·83	24·17	79	13·17	65·83	129	21·50	107·50	179	29·83	149·17	229	38·17	190·83	279	46·50	232·50
30	5·00	25·00	80	13·33	66·67	130	21·67	108·33	180	30·00	150·00	230	38·33	191·67	280	46·67	233·33
31	5·17	25·83	81	13·50	67·50	131	21·83	109·17	181	30·17	150·83	231	38·50	192·50	281	46·83	234·17
32	5·33	26·67	82	13·67	68·33	132	22·00	110·00	182	30·33	151·67	232	38·67	193·33	282	47·00	235·00
33	5·50	27·50	83	13·83	69·17	133	22·17	110·83	183	30·50	152·50	233	38·83	194·17	283	47·17	235·83
34	5·67	28·33	84	14·00	70·00	134	22·33	111·67	184	30·67	153·33	234	39·00	195·00	284	47·33	236·67
35	5·83	29·17	85	14·17	70·83	135	22·50	112·50	185	30·83	154·17	235	39·17	195·83	285	47·50	237·50
36	6·00	30·00	86	14·33	71·67	136	22·67	113·33	186	31·00	155·00	236	39·33	196·67	286	47·67	238·33
37	6·17	30·83	87	14·50	72·50	137	22·83	114·17	187	31·17	155·83	237	39·50	197·50	287	47·83	239·17
38	6·33	31·67	88	14·67	73·33	138	23·00	115·00	188	31·33	156·67	238	39·67	198·33	288	48·00	240·00
39	6·50	32·50	89	14·83	74·17	139	23·17	115·83	189	31·50	157·50	239	39·83	199·17	289	48·17	240·83
40	6·67	33·33	90	15·00	75·00	140	23·33	116·67	190	31·67	158·33	240	40·00	200·00	290	48·33	241·67
41	6·83	34·17	91	15·17	75·83	141	23·50	117·50	191	31·83	159·17	241	40·17	200·83	291	48·50	242·50
42	7·00	35·00	92	15·33	76·67	142	23·67	118·33	192	32·00	160·00	242	40·33	201·67	292	48·67	243·33
43	7·17	35·83	93	15·50	77·50	143	23·83	119·17	193	32·17	160·83	243	40·50	202·50	293	48·83	244·17
44	7·33	36·67	94	15·67	78·33	144	24·00	120·00	194	32·33	161·67	244	40·67	203·33	294	49·00	245·00
45	7·50	37·50	95	15·83	79·17	145	24·17	120·83	195	32·50	162·50	245	40·83	204·17	295	49·17	245·83
46	7·67	38·33	96	16·00	80·00	146	24·33	121·67	196	32·67	163·33	246	41·00	205·00	296	49·33	246·67
47	7·83	39·17	97	16·17	80·83	147	24·50	122·50	197	32·83	164·17	247	41·17	205·83	297	49·50	247·50
48	8·00	40·00	98	16·33	81·67	148	24·67	123·33	198	33·00	165·00	248	41·33	206·67	298	49·67	248·33
49	8·17	40·83	99	16·50	82·50	149	24·83	124·17	199	33·17	165·83	249	41·50	207·50	299	49·83	249·17
50	8·33	41·67	100	16·67	83·33	150	25·00	125·00	200	33·33	166·67	250	41·67	208·33	300	50·00	250·00
500	83·33	416·67	600	100·00	500·00	700	116·67	583·33	800	133·33	666·67	900	150·00	750·00	1,000	166·67	833·33

Number of days Table: Tax Year

Years other than leap years

(Quarter days are highlighted)

Days	April lapsed	to go	May lapsed	to go	June lapsed	to go	July lapsed	to go	August lapsed	to go	September lapsed	to go	October lapsed	to go	November lapsed	to go	December lapsed	to go	January lapsed	to go	February lapsed	to go	March lapsed	to go	Days
1	361	4	26	339	57	308	87	278	118	247	149	216	179	186	210	155	240	125	271	94	302	63	330	35	1
2	362	3	27	338	58	307	88	277	119	246	150	215	180	185	211	154	241	124	272	93	303	62	331	34	2
3	363	2	28	337	59	306	89	276	120	245	151	214	181	184	212	153	242	123	273	92	304	61	332	33	3
4	364	1	29	336	60	305	90	275	121	244	152	213	182	183	213	152	243	122	274	91	305	60	333	32	4
5	365	0	30	335	61	304	91	274	122	243	153	212	183	182	214	151	244	121	275	90	306	59	334	31	5
6	1	364	31	334	62	303	92	273	123	242	154	211	184	181	215	150	245	120	276	89	307	58	335	30	6
7	2	363	32	333	63	302	93	272	124	241	155	210	185	180	216	149	246	119	277	88	308	57	336	29	7
8	3	362	33	332	64	301	94	271	125	240	156	209	186	179	217	148	247	118	278	87	309	56	337	28	8
9	4	361	34	331	65	300	95	270	126	239	157	208	187	178	218	147	248	117	279	86	310	55	338	27	9
10	5	360	35	330	66	299	96	269	127	238	158	207	188	177	219	146	249	116	280	85	311	54	339	26	10
11	6	359	36	329	67	298	97	268	128	237	159	206	189	176	220	145	250	115	281	84	312	53	340	25	11
12	7	358	37	328	68	297	98	267	129	236	160	205	190	175	221	144	251	114	282	83	313	52	341	24	12
13	8	357	38	327	69	296	99	266	130	235	161	204	191	174	222	143	252	113	283	82	314	51	342	23	13
14	9	356	39	326	70	295	100	265	131	234	162	203	192	173	223	142	253	112	284	81	315	50	343	22	14
15	10	355	40	325	71	294	101	264	132	233	163	202	193	172	224	141	254	111	285	80	316	49	344	21	15
16	11	354	41	324	72	293	102	263	133	232	164	201	194	171	225	140	255	110	286	79	317	48	345	20	16
17	12	353	42	323	73	292	103	262	134	231	165	200	195	170	226	139	256	109	287	78	318	47	346	19	17
18	13	352	43	322	74	291	104	261	135	230	166	199	196	169	227	138	257	108	288	77	319	46	347	18	18
19	14	351	44	321	75	290	105	260	136	229	167	198	197	168	228	137	258	107	289	76	320	45	348	17	19
20	15	350	45	320	76	289	106	259	137	228	168	197	198	167	229	136	259	106	290	75	321	44	349	16	20
21	16	349	46	319	77	288	107	258	138	227	169	196	199	166	230	135	260	105	291	74	322	43	350	15	21
22	17	348	47	318	78	287	108	257	139	226	170	195	200	165	231	134	261	104	292	73	323	42	351	14	22
23	18	347	48	317	79	286	109	256	140	225	171	194	201	164	232	133	262	103	293	72	324	41	352	13	23
24	19	346	49	316	80	285	110	255	141	224	172	193	202	163	233	132	263	102	294	71	325	40	353	12	24
25	20	345	50	315	81	284	111	254	142	223	173	192	203	162	234	131	264	101	295	70	326	39	354	11	25
26	21	344	51	314	82	283	112	253	143	222	174	191	204	161	235	130	265	100	296	69	327	38	355	10	26
27	22	343	52	313	83	282	113	252	144	221	175	190	205	160	236	129	266	99	297	68	328	37	356	9	27
28	23	342	53	312	84	281	114	251	145	220	176	189	206	159	237	128	267	98	298	67	329	36	357	8	28
29	24	341	54	311	85	280	115	250	146	219	177	188	207	158	238	127	268	97	299	66			358	7	29
30	25	340	55	310	86	279	116	249	147	218	178	187	208	157	239	126	269	96	300	65			359	6	30
31			56	309			117	248	148	217			209	156			270	95	301	64			360	5	31

Number of days Table: Tax Year

Leap years falling within tax years 2015/16   2019/2020   2023/24   (Quarter days are highlighted)

Days	April lapsed	April to go	May lapsed	May to go	June lapsed	June to go	July lapsed	July to go	August lapsed	August to go	September lapsed	September to go	October lapsed	October to go	November lapsed	November to go	December lapsed	December to go	January lapsed	January to go	February lapsed	February to go	March lapsed	March to go	Days
1	362	4	26	340	57	309	87	279	118	248	149	217	179	187	210	156	240	126	271	95	302	64	331	35	1
2	363	3	27	339	58	308	88	278	119	247	150	216	180	186	211	155	241	125	272	94	303	63	332	34	2
3	364	2	28	338	59	307	89	277	120	246	151	215	181	185	212	154	242	124	273	93	304	62	333	33	3
4	365	1	29	337	60	306	90	276	121	245	152	214	182	184	213	153	243	123	274	92	305	61	334	32	4
5	366	0	30	336	61	305	91	275	122	244	153	213	183	183	214	152	244	122	275	91	306	60	335	31	5
6	1	365	31	335	62	304	92	274	123	243	154	212	184	182	215	151	245	121	276	90	307	59	336	30	6
7	2	364	32	334	63	303	93	273	124	242	155	211	185	181	216	150	246	120	277	89	308	58	337	29	7
8	3	363	33	333	64	302	94	272	125	241	156	210	186	180	217	149	247	119	278	88	309	57	338	28	8
9	4	362	34	332	65	301	95	271	126	240	157	209	187	179	218	148	248	118	279	87	310	56	339	27	9
10	5	361	35	331	66	300	96	270	127	239	158	208	188	178	219	147	249	117	280	86	311	55	340	26	10
11	6	360	36	330	67	299	97	269	128	238	159	207	189	177	220	146	250	116	281	85	312	54	341	25	11
12	7	359	37	329	68	298	98	268	129	237	160	206	190	176	221	145	251	115	282	84	313	53	342	24	12
13	8	358	38	328	69	297	99	267	130	236	161	205	191	175	222	144	252	114	283	83	314	52	343	23	13
14	9	357	39	327	70	296	100	266	131	235	162	204	192	174	223	143	253	113	284	82	315	51	344	22	14
15	10	356	40	326	71	295	101	265	132	234	163	203	193	173	224	142	254	112	285	81	316	50	345	21	15
16	11	355	41	325	72	294	102	264	133	233	164	202	194	172	225	141	255	111	286	80	317	49	346	20	16
17	12	354	42	324	73	293	103	263	134	232	165	201	195	171	226	140	256	110	287	79	318	48	347	19	17
18	13	353	43	323	74	292	104	262	135	231	166	200	196	170	227	139	257	109	288	78	319	47	348	18	18
19	14	352	44	322	75	291	105	261	136	230	167	199	197	169	228	138	258	108	289	77	320	46	349	17	19
20	15	351	45	321	76	290	106	260	137	229	168	198	198	168	229	137	259	107	290	76	321	45	350	16	20
21	16	350	46	320	77	289	107	259	138	228	169	197	199	167	230	136	260	106	291	75	322	44	351	15	21
22	17	349	47	319	78	288	108	258	139	227	170	196	200	166	231	135	261	105	292	74	323	43	352	14	22
23	18	348	48	318	79	287	109	257	140	226	171	195	201	165	232	134	262	104	293	73	324	42	353	13	23
24	19	347	49	317	80	286	110	256	141	225	172	194	202	164	233	133	263	103	294	72	325	41	354	12	24
25	20	346	50	316	81	285	111	255	142	224	173	193	203	163	234	132	264	102	295	71	326	40	355	11	25
26	21	345	51	315	82	284	112	254	143	223	174	192	204	162	235	131	265	101	296	70	327	39	356	10	26
27	22	344	52	314	83	283	113	253	144	222	175	191	205	161	236	130	266	100	297	69	328	38	357	9	27
28	23	343	53	313	84	282	114	252	145	221	176	190	206	160	237	129	267	99	298	68	329	37	358	8	28
29	24	342	54	312	85	281	115	251	146	220	177	189	207	159	238	128	268	98	299	67	330	36	359	7	29
30	25	341	55	311	86	280	116	250	147	219	178	188	208	158	239	127	269	97	300	66			360	6	30
31			56	310			117	249	148	218			209	157			270	96	301	65			361	5	31

Tax Year Planner 2015/16

	April	May	June	July	August	Sept	Oct	Nov	Dec	Jan	Feb	March	April	
Mon			1								1	1		Mon
Tue			2			1			1		2	2		Tue
Wed	1		3	1		2			2		3	3		Wed
Thurs	2		4	2		3	1		3		4	4	1	Thurs
Fri	3	1	5	3		4	2		4	1	5	5	2	Fri
Sat	4	2	6	4	1	5	3		5	2	6	6	3	Sat
Sun	5	3	7	5	2	6	4	1	6	3	7	7	4	Sun
Mon	6	4	8	6	3	7	5	2	7	4	8	8	5	Mon
Tue	7	5	9	7	4	8	6	3	8	5	9	9	6	Tue
Wed	8	6	10	8	5	9	7	4	9	6	10	10	7	Wed
Thurs	9	7	11	9	6	10	8	5	10	7	11	11	8	Thurs
Fri	10	8	12	10	7	11	9	6	11	8	12	12	9	Fri
Sat	11	9	13	11	8	12	10	7	12	9	13	13	10	Sat
Sun	12	10	14	12	9	13	11	8	13	10	14	14	11	Sun
Mon	13	11	15	13	10	14	12	9	14	11	15	15	12	Mon
Tue	14	12	16	14	11	15	13	10	15	12	16	16	13	Tue
Wed	15	13	17	15	12	16	14	11	16	13	17	17	14	Wed
Thurs	16	14	18	16	13	17	15	12	17	14	18	18	15	Thurs
Fri	17	15	19	17	14	18	16	13	18	15	19	19	16	Fri
Sat	18	16	20	18	15	19	17	14	19	16	20	20	17	Sat
Sun	19	17	21	19	16	20	18	15	20	17	21	21	18	Sun
Mon	20	18	22	20	17	21	19	16	21	18	22	22	19	Mon
Tue	21	19	23	21	18	22	20	17	22	19	23	23	20	Tue
Wed	22	20	24	22	19	23	21	18	23	20	24	24	21	Wed
Thurs	23	21	25	23	20	24	22	19	24	21	25	25	22	Thurs
Fri	24	22	26	24	21	25	23	20	25	22	26	26	23	Fri
Sat	25	23	27	25	22	26	24	21	26	23	27	27	24	Sat
Sun	26	24	28	26	23	27	25	22	27	24	28	28	25	Sun
Mon	27	25	29	27	24	28	26	23	28	25		29	26	Mon
Tue	28	26	30	28	25	29	27	24	29	26		30	27	Tue
Wed	29	27		29	26	30	28	25	30	27		31	28	Wed
Thurs	30	28		30	27		29	26	31	28			29	Thurs
Fri		29		31	28		30	27		29			30	Fri
Sat		30			29		31	28		30				Sat
Sun		31			30			29		31				Sun
Mon					31			30						Mon
Tue														Tue